CANOE TRIPS
BRITISH COLUMBIA

The Essential Guidebook for Novice and
Intermediate Canoeists and Kayakers. Covers
95 Daytrips and Wilderness Camping Trips.

by Jack Wainwright

Distributed by **Gordon Soules Book
Publishers Ltd**. ● 1354-B Marine Drive,
West Vancouver BC Canada V7T 1B5
● 620-1916 Pike Place, Seattle WA 98101 US
E-mail: books@gordonsoules.com
Web site: http://www.gordonsoules.com
(604) 922 6588 Fax: (604) 688 5442

WAINBAY
ENTERPRISES

Box 115, Abbotsford, B.C., Canada, V2S 4N8
Tel: (604) 853-9320 Fax: (604) 852-6933

Canadian Cataloguing in Publication Data

Wainwright, Jack, 1933-
  Canoe Trips British Columbia

ISBN 1-896217-00-1

1. Canoes and canoeing – British Columbia – Guidebooks.
2. Kayaking – British Columbia – Guidebooks. 3. Camping –
British Columbia – Guidebooks. 4. British Columbia –
Guidebooks. I. Title.
GV776.15.B7W34 1994   797.1'22'09711   C94-910472-8

Published in Canada by:

Wainbay Enterprises
Box 115
Abbotsford, B.C.
V2S 4N8
(604) 853-9320

Distributed by **Gordon Soules Book Publishers Ltd.** ● 1354-B Marine Drive, West Vancouver BC Canada V7T 1B5 ● 620-1916 Pike Place, Seattle WA 98101 US E-mail: books@gordonsoules.com Web site: http://www.gordonsoules.com (604) 922 6588 Fax: (604) 688 5442

Typeset in Canada by Summit Productions
Printed and bound in Canada by Friesens Corporation
Cover design by Talent Graphics Studio (604) 584-5966
Map printed by Friesens Corporation

First printing: 1994
Second printing: 1995
Third printing: 1997

Front cover Photo:
*Paddling Picture Lake near the B.C. – Washington border
by Marlin Bayes, Western Canoeing Inc.*
(604) 853-9320

Disclaimer

This guidebook is intended to provide basic information on canoeing and kayaking British Columbia waters. It is designed to help you have safe and enjoyable paddling experiences. The book is sold with the understanding that neither the author nor publisher is engaged in professional teaching and guiding services. It is intended to augment and complement instruction available through paddling clubs and private and public courses. It should be used as a general guide to help paddlers decide where and when to go and how to get there.

The author has done exhaustive research to give complete and accurate information on each destination but paddlers should be aware that paddling and access conditions may change dramatically from day-to-day, season-to-season, and year-to-year. The enclosed map should be used for general reference only and is not suitable for navigation.

Publisher's Notes

A Passion for Paddling

It's dawn. I'm standing alone on a finger of land that juts into Coaster Channel in the Broken Islands. The cool sea air is spiced with the delicate scent of cedar and salt. Beside me a huge cedar leans over the still water peering at its own reflection. Somewhere in the forest behind me an eagle calls. His lonely lament goes unanswered. A few yards down the beach a solitary crow clucks and swaggers along the high tide line searching for breakfast. Here and there across the channel, wisps of mist hang above the water like ghosts.

To the east a familiar black shape rounds a distant point. I cup my hands and squint into the early sun. The shape travels slowly across the dazzling slash of sunlight. It takes a moment before I see that it is not a killer whale at all, but a lone canoeist. From this distance he seems suspended between heaven and earth, diamonds dripping from his paddle.

Dawn in the Broken Islands. Marlin Bayes photo.

This scene, or ones very much like it, occur most every day throughout spring, summer, fall and even winter in British Columbia. This province is a paddler's paradise. In fact, some of us find it difficult to believe that B.C.'s geography is the result of millions of years of evolution and not the design of some clever landscape architect who had a passion for paddling.

We are blessed here with some of the finest canoeing and kayaking waters on the planet. We produced this book in the hope that it will aid you as you set out to discover them for yourself.

A word of caution: Paddle sports can be deadly for the ill-prepared or poorly-equipped. Only a fool would venture onto these waters without ensuring that their equipment and skills are adequate for the task. If you are a beginner, we urge that you join a paddling club, take lessons and learn to honestly assess your paddling abilities. Although many experienced paddlers do travel alone we stand by the admonition that three canoes make a safe trip.

The single most important item you can take along on any of these trips is common sense. Apply it liberally whether you're out for an evening paddle on a local pond or embarking on a week-long expedition.

For novice and intermediate paddlers, we offer this book as a comprehensive guide to many of B.C.'s favorite paddling destinations.

We hope the book recalls memories of fine summer days for those who have traveled some of these waters.

We also hope it will motivate non-paddlers to experience canoe or kayak tripping. Once you hear the rhythmic dip and splash of a paddle you will never again view water in quite the same way. You will find yourself gazing across bays and inlets wondering what lies around the next bend. You will never again pass by some stream or river without wondering if it could be run.

And finally, we hope, you will add your voice to the chorus of paddlers who have worked so hard, and successfully, to protect the world's wild places.

Doug Brunt
May, 1994

CONTENTS

Acknowledgements

It is one thing to have been on a trip and write up your experiences and quite another to write them up for others to follow. There are so many variables ranging from weather conditions, to water levels that it is impossible for any one person to be up to date on all these trips.

With that in mind, we called several active paddlers in various parts of B.C. All were happy to share their knowledge to help make this book as current as possible.

To my wife Elise, who has been my bow paddler on most of these trips, I give special thanks. Her editorial help has been invaluable. A special thanks also goes to Mary Bayes for her editorial assistance.

Our thanks to Wally Priedolins and Heather Spain for combing through our coast trips and sharing personal experiences and concerns.

Our northern trips were reviewed by Lyle Dickieson, Prince George; Dave McCulloch, Quesnel and Geerd VanderMeulen, Telkwa. Their experiences and that of other paddlers up there were invaluable in being as current as possible.

Bill Dudas, Kamloops, is a retired geologist who added suggestions for his area of expertise.

George Appel, Bert Port and Brian Miller from Castlegar and Creston reviewed it for the waters they paddle as did Chris Cooper of Cooper Graphics, Pitt Meadows.

Thanks to Dogwood Canoe Club members Olaf Olsen, Jean Allen, Elaine Wismer, Dan Wainwright, Dinty Moore, Jack Apps, Esther and Martin Kafer, Adolf Teufle and Frans Vanlakerveld.

Suggestions also came from Brian Creer, Dave Stevens, Darcy O'Shea, Bill Kent, Mary and Marlin Bayes and Lynne Smith. A very special thanks goes to all RCA members for their help and support in compiling the manuscript. There is no way of remembering all the little conversations with active paddlers over the years which also helped to shape this book, but credit goes to them too.

In fact so much help from the active paddling community went into this book, I can no longer consider it mine. It really belongs to all the contributors. Thanks for your help.

Jack Wainwright

Organized Paddling in B.C.

In the early '60s, organized canoeing in British Columbia came of age. Dinty Moore, a paddler and owner of Moore's Sales in Vancouver imported the famous eastern Chestnut line of quality wood/canvas canoes and the indestructible aluminum Grumman canoes.

B.C. had its own quality canoe builder in Sid Greenwood of Richmond. Many of these classic boats are still in use today in 1994. Dinty and Sid met and discussed the need for a canoeing organization to promote safety and the recreational use of canoes. In one year in the mid 60's, 54 small boaters drowned in B.C. Clearly there was a need for education. In 1964 Dinty collected names at the boat show and initiated a meeting of recreational paddlers which met in his home municipality of Burnaby.

They called themselves the Dogwood Canoe Club. The Dogwoodies almost by default became the backbone of organized canoeing in the lower mainland.

In 1965 Dinty and Frans Vanlakerveld participated in the inaugural meetings of what was to become Canoe Sport B.C., the governing body for canoeing in the province. There were strong clubs in Victoria, Prince George and Kamloops, but because Canoe Sport was based on the mainland, the Dogwood C.C. provided most of the energy for the new Recreational Canoeing Association of B. C. branch of CSBC. Dinty believed that no commercially involved person should serve on the executive because there was a potential conflict of interest. He therefore elected to remain off the executive but act as catalyst and support behind the scenes. DCCers Frans Vanlakerveld and Bill Wilson were table officers.These organizations were primarily formed in response to government grants being available for sports. The grants, however, were initially aimed more at competitive paddling than recreational enjoyment and safety.

In 1967 a paddler of extraordinary energy and commitment appeared on the scene. Brian Creer, (another Dogwoodie), has become a legend. Brian held many administrative positions in CSBC, RCA of

BC, and the Whitewater Association of Kayakers. And even today, he is the person to call if you have questions on canoeing in B.C. One of his phone lines is exclusively for Canoeing business. In recognition of his efforts he was one of only five people ever awarded life membership in the Recreational Canoeing Association of B.C. The others were Jack Akins (Victoria CC), Dinty Moore (DCC), Jack Wainwright (DCC) and Dave Stevens (Association of Neighborhood Houses).

In the late 1960s, Faye Eccelston of the "Y" through CSBC initiated a survey of members to gather information on canoeing trips in B.C. This first trip guide was just mimeographed pages stapled together, but it was a start. It eventually was published in book form by Nunaga Publishing.

In the very early '70s, RCA was experiencing difficulties trying to represent the whole province, initiate instructional and safety programs and compete with the racing paddlers for a share of grant money. Once again the Dogwoodies responded with new energy. Bob Lornie, Wally Priedolins, Keith Spain, Jeff Wisdom, Gerry Lamb, Karen Adams, Des Winterbottom, Betty Donaldson, Rick Bryan, Jim Lindsay and Jack Wainwright waded into the fray. In 1975 the RCA executive was made up of Adolf Teufele from Kamloops, Jack Akins of Victoria and four DCCers. The direction they took was to promote safety and recreational enjoyment.

In 1973, experienced paddlers met at Paradise Valley to qualify individuals as canoeing instructors. Paddling courses were then written. The first basic course was put in print following an historic weekend session in Hope B.C. by Kamloops paddlers Harvey Fraser and Adolf Teufele and Dogwoodies Dinty Moore and Jack Wainwright. Brian Creer taught and improved this first course in the new outdoor program at Capilano College. Brian White of Capilano College was a pioneer in providing serious courses for Outdoor Recreation in B.C. Many Cap College graduates have gone on to make major contributions to our sport. Among the most prominent are John Hatchard who was RCA of BC instructor-coordinator for many years and Tynke Braaksma, who has been an active member of the RCA of BC executive.

Eventually a series of courses were developed for different paddling conditions. They had significant influence on the courses later developed by the Canadian Recreational Canoeing Association and modified for use across Canada. Dave Stevens was awarded life membership for, among other things, his major contribution in developing a comprehensive instructional manual.

The energy of organized paddling was being spent on instruction and competition. When time came to update the Trip Guide, they could not do it and so let their rights go to private interests. Richard and Rochelle Wright published the very informative Canoe Routes British Columbia (1977, 1980). This book has been out of print for several years now and will not be reprinted by the publishers.

The number of recreational paddlers has increased significantly. In 1976 the DCC decided it was time for a second lower mainland canoe club. President Jack Wainwright and Neil Dockendorf of Burnaby Parks Board initiated a meeting of Burnaby Parks canoe classes and with input from the DCC, the Beaver Canoe Club was born. Dogwoodies and Beavers paddle the lower mainland waters every week. Club members have also wilderness tripped all over B.C. There is a wealth of paddling information locked up in their experiences.

A major factor in the increase in canoeing in recent years has been the emergence of a quality canoe builder once again. Marlin Bayes and Mary Bayes (more ex Dogwoodies) own Western Canoeing in Abbotsford where they specialize in fiberglass and other modern materials in the design and manufacture of canoes. Their recognized expertise and marketing skills have won them markets internationally. Lynne Smith, Western Canoeing's sales manager has been tireless in her promotion of organized recreational paddling. She is a strong influence in the Valley Paddlers' Club, has served on the RCA of BC executive for many years and is regularly organizing public promotional events.

The early RCA executives deliberately held meetings outside the lower mainland in an effort to encourage full provincial participation. For many years the executive has not been dominated by any one group which is a healthy sign that recreational canoeing has come of age in B.C.

We now have many more Canoe Clubs around the province. Many have been quietly enjoying the sport in their area with little recognition provincially. In our appendix we have included the current list of Recreational Canoe Clubs of B.C.

We need new print material on where to canoe in B.C., not only for tourists and those new to the sport, but to help spread the action around so that a few well publicized routes do not get over-used. So, once again we are using the experiences of organized paddlers to produce a summary of recreational paddling locations in B.C. The publisher, Summit Productions, is owned by Doug Brunt, another avid paddler who recognizes the need for this book.

The author, Jack Wainwright has been involved in canoeing at both club and provincial levels since 1972. He has been awarded lifetime membership in the RCA of BC.

We hope you find this book useful. It was written to fill a void and act as a guide for the enjoyment of recreational canoeing. We would urge everyone to join a club or at least get some instruction in how to paddle safely. If you cannot paddle a canoe 100 meters in a straight line without changing paddling sides, you could use some instruction. If you have never rescued or been rescued, get the experience before you need it!

Clubs are not for everyone. However, they give everyone a good start toward a safe, enjoyable paddling experience.

May the winds always favor you.

Jack Wainwright
January 2, 1994

Canoeing in B.C.

British Columbia has the most diverse, unspoiled and interesting geography in North America. Most people only see it from a distance or through the window of a speeding car. Paddlers know it and enjoy it in an unhurried stress-free way. Remote rivers meander through valleys now as they did when the last ice age receded more than 10,000 years ago. There are still areas unimproved by man...no roads, no railroads, no power poles, with spectacular scenery and unconcerned wildlife. The occasional decaying log cabin may be the only reminder that others have preceded you.

Most canoe campers now practise no-trace camping and not only pack refuse out or bury it, but also will scatter the fire rings of earlier campers left behind out of ignorance rather than thoughtlessness. We want to maintain the magic.

The very remoteness and often very cold water make it imperative that paddlers in B.C. take special precautions. If you have taken canoeing lessons, you will know how difficult it is to rescue yourself if you dump. The condition that caused the upset hinders a self rescue. You will also know how quickly another experienced paddler can rescue you.

Our rule of thumb is **three canoes make a safe trip**.

Many people do paddle alone without difficulty, but in B.C.'s cold water your first mistake may well be your last.

If in doubt, plunge your hand in over the wrist and count how many seconds you can hold it there. Then realize that you lose half your strength when you get immersed in cold water because the blood supply to your limbs is reduced as your body tries to maintain body temperature in the torso. You will then understand why B.C. paddlers die every year in the spring and fall. Invariably they were paddling with only one canoe in cold water.

Organized paddlers in B.C. recommend carrying more gear than the legal limit.

MINIMUM CANOEING GEAR REQUIRED BY LAW

MOT approved PFD (personal flotation device) 1 per person in the boat. This may be a cushion or vest.

PADDLES one per person to two per boat.

BAILER one container that can scoop out water.

PAINTERS (ropes) attached bow and stern.

SOUND SIGNAL (Horn)

LIGHT at night; an intermittent flashlight is ok.

RECOMMENDED ADDITIONAL CANOEING GEAR

Vest Type PFD worn while in the canoe.

SOUND SIGNAL: a loud whistle that works when wet , attached to PFD.

A spare PADDLE

BAILER not tied in. (make a scoop from a bleach bottle).

PAINTERS 8 mm (3/8") floating line as long as the canoe but not over 8 m 25 ft. long; attached bow and stern; coiled for use; no knots or attachments.

A CHANGE OF CLOTHES and **MATCHES** in waterproof containers.

Pastoral paddling in the Fraser Valley. Marlin Bayes photo.

Tips on Choosing
Your Equipment

If you are in the market for a canoe, be aware that there is a bewildering assortment of designs and materials. A beginner will be happiest with a canoe that tracks well so he is less at the mercy of the wind. A shallow arch hull over 30 cm (12 in.) deep will provide enough freeboard and stability. A 3.75 m (16 ft.) boat is the minimum length for a general purpose canoe. The canoe should have a strong bottom to resist "oil-canning". A well-made fiberglass canoe meeting these conditions will weigh 30-34 kg (70 to 75 lbs.). If you do not understand this jargon you will at least know the questions to ask when you visit a dealer.

Choosing a paddle is also bewildering. So is the price range. The inexpensive plastic and aluminum "Mohawk" is used in the rental trade and will take lots of abuse. Laminated wood blades are preferred by many. Choose a straight shaft if you are a beginner. The bent shafts have only one power face and take more getting used to. Correct paddle length will depend on how long your torso is and how high your canoe seats are above water level. Generally a length of 51 in. to 54 in. will suit most people.

Your PFD (Personal Flotation Device) must fit comfortably and not bind your arms or chest when paddling. All Ministry Of Transport approved PFDs have sufficient buoyancy to float anyone. Paddlers with short torsos are most comfortable in short vests. When you try it on for fit, sit in a canoe or on a low stool to make sure it does not bunch or push up when you sit. The PFD is a piece of clothing and fit, not price, should be the determining factor in buying.

Transporting your canoe used to be easy when all vehicles had rain drip rails. Now there are roof racks that are custom rigged for your vehicle. They adapt to carry bikes, canoes, kayaks, skiis....all for a price. The least expensive car top adaptation are foam blocks that snap on to the gunnels (top rim of canoe) and cushion it when you put it on the car. However if sand gets under them they may not be such a bargain given the price of even minor auto body work these days.

Once your canoe is on your vehicle, it is essential that it be tied properly. Most damage to canoes is not caused when using them, but when transporting them. They fly off in traffic!

Check your tie-down system against the diagram. Remember that today's vehicles are often shorter than the canoe and may need an extra rope restraining forward travel in sudden stops. If you are using your painters to tie-down, the **Trucker's Hitch** is the preferred knot to eliminate permanent knots in your painters.

The author ties one on. Bow and Stern ropes tied as V-shapes minimize wind deflection. Rope (not bungy) secures canoe to roof racks. Knots on passenger side let you retie in safety on the road. Use the Trucker's Hitch for all four tie-downs. This knot is so effective, it can bend your boat if it is too tight. Doug Brunt Photo.

Trucker's Hitch - Used to cinch a load tightly to its vehicle and leave no permanent knot in the rope.

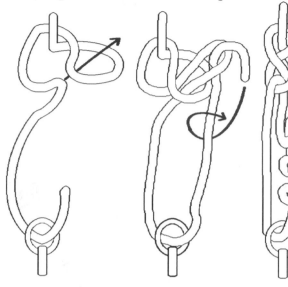

1. Lay tie-down rope in place.
2. Twist main part of rope to make a loop.
3. Pull another small loop from the main rope below the twist through the first loop.
4. Thread the end of the rope through the second loop and pull tight, cinching the load down.
5. Secure the cinch with two half-hitches.

Bowline

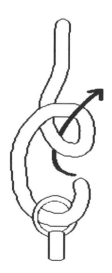

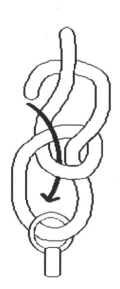

Used to form a non-slip, non-jamming loop in the end of a rope. Twist a loop in the main part of the rope then feed the end of the rope through the loop, around the main rope and back down through the loop. Pull tight leaving a loop in the end of the rope.

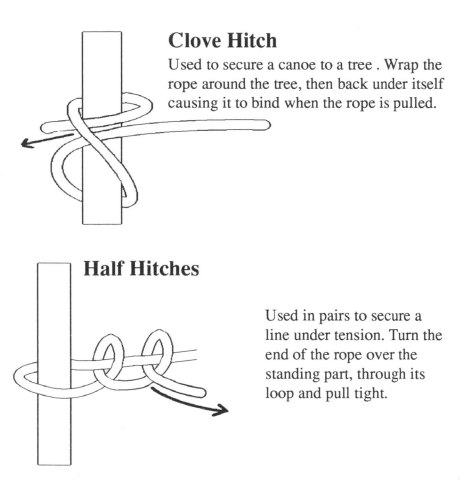

Clove Hitch

Used to secure a canoe to a tree . Wrap the rope around the tree, then back under itself causing it to bind when the rope is pulled.

Half Hitches

Used in pairs to secure a line under tension. Turn the end of the rope over the standing part, through its loop and pull tight.

Figure Eight knot

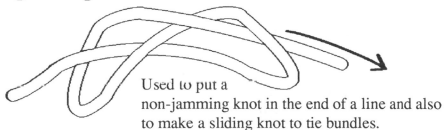

Used to put a non-jamming knot in the end of a line and also to make a sliding knot to tie bundles.

Tips for Day Tripping

CLOTHING

Dress for the weather expected but also realize that the unexpected must always be anticipated. Leave the rain gear at home and you are sure to entice a thunder shower. You may be up to 100 miles from home and several hours from shelter. The micro-climate you are paddling in may not have the same weather as home. Be prepared.

Extra sized rain parkas or water repellent nylon shells can be worn over your PFD. The PFD stays dry and provides a bit of insulation too. Keep your head covered. The combination of sun and water can give severe burns. Long sleeves ward off sunburn and mosquitoes. Wool and the new synthetic fleeces insulate even when wet....just wring them out and put them on. Denim blue jeans may be hard wearing, but they wick heat away when wet and take forever to dry. The stretch jeans, cotton drills, and wool are better insulators and dry quicker. GORE•TEX® is a space age fabric that lets perspiration escape and keeps rain out. While expensive, GORE•TEX® clothing will give you a much sunnier outlook.

FOOTWEAR can be a problem as in the normal course of events, you will probably get your feet wet. On day trips, many paddlers just wear wool socks and running shoes and have wet feet. Many times I have not bothered to change to dry at trip's end because I was not uncomfortable. Some wear wetsuit boots which have thicker soles for walking on gravel bars. The best of these have easy-access zippers. Others wear the waterproof footwear they normally use when canoe camping such as yachting boots, gum boots, waterproof hiking boots or waterproof hightop workboots. These keep your feet dry but are difficult to swim in if you dump.

Pack a change of clothes and a towel in a waterproof container and carry it in the canoe.

WATERPROOF CONTAINERS come in a wide range of shapes and sizes. Canoe dealers carry an assortment of waterproof bags, some with backpack straps. The large 20 l (5 gal.) plastic buckets with reusable lids are popular as they stow well and can be used as seats around camp. They can be found at some canoe dealers, paint suppliers or scrounged used from restaurants. Test them for waterproofness by immersing them in the bathtub. Used ones may leak. Bucket lids are hard to remove, but there is a removal tool available. Use one bucket for emergency change of clothes and raingear. Use a second one for lunch, first-aid kit, sun screen, insect repellent and the like. Do NOT rely on garbage bags to keep things dry.

Canoes are often stolen off cars or from homes. Lock it with a bicycle cable to something secure. I use 2 m (6 ft.) stranded bike cables looped around a thwart and padlocked to my tow hitch. Of course I didn't start that until I had one stolen off my car.

The well-appointed paddler. Jack Wainwright photo.

Paddling with Children

Canoeing familes share quality time and memorable experiences. Many start with babes-in-carriers and progress to proficient young paddlers. Others have their children rebel at canoeing as they get older. The reason may well be that just being a passenger and being told to sit still does not generate any enthusiasm. Children everywhere try to emulate their parents and try very hard to become proficient at whatever adults do.

In our canoe club, children are often on all but the most challenging trips. The key to happy young paddlers is just that; let them paddle. That is easier said than done, however. Young children are neither ready nor strong enough to take over the bow or stern. They have to start paddling from their seat in the middle section and therein lies the problem. Paddling at the broadest part of the canoe and sitting at the centerline forces the youngster to do an awkward sweep stroke. It throws the steering off and often the child's paddle hits the adult's paddle thus interfering with comfortable cruising. The seating must be modified to let the child sit beside a gunwale, off the centerline. Paddles must be sized to the child. Child paddles range from 36 to 48 in. After that, go to the shortest, lightest adult paddle.

In canoes with a foot brace, the brace can be replaced with a 1x10 board to form a bench seat. All canoes can have seat brackets installed to accommodate a similar bench seat anywhere there is adequate leg room for the paddler. A temporary bench seat can be made by cutting three-inch-thick, high-density, closed-cell foam to conform to the canoe's curves at the chine (water-line) and gluing one on each end of a 1x10 board. The height of the child's seat must be low enough to maintain a low center of gravity for the canoe, yet high enough for the child to paddle comfortably. The optimum height will be close to half the depth of the canoe amidships. It goes without saying that you will have to balance the load so the canoe is in trim and floats evenly side to side and front and back.

Many commercially available canoe passenger seats force the

passenger to sit astride the centerline to make the craft more stable, but it also prevents comfortable paddling and for children, that translates into BORRRRING!

When our kids were young, my brother-in law and I canoe camped at Murtle Lake in Wells Gray Park. Bill's youngest boys, Chris and Scott shared the broad bench bow seat of their Frontiersman. One was left handed, the other right so it worked out well. In fact with those two little motors in front, Bill had little more to do than steer. The year the bunch of us canoe camped on Azure and Clearwater lakes, our kids were proficient enough to handle their own canoes. We had seven kids, two adults and four canoes. The only problem was portaging up the river as we couldn't paddle it. A potential tough slog for the two Dads...until we hired a boat to run us up. Where there's a will, there's a way.

My oldest son, Dan, and I paddled together on many day trips and wilderness excursions. He became the youngest RCA canoeing instructor and caused a rule change making 16 the youngest age anyone could qualify for instructor certification. He is now paddling with his children, and has been on our canoe club executive for years.

Start'em young. Marlin Bayes photo.

Small Lakes

Within a few hours drive of Vancouver

There are many small lakes throughout B.C.; some remote, some very accessible. The ones we are listing are accessible and often popular. They offer the beginning or casual canoeist a generally safe and enjoyable paddling experience. In summer, the presence of other paddlers provides a safety measure in the case of upset. The few small boating fatalities on these waters almost always are alcohol related. Power boats are frequently restricted which adds to the peace of a day's paddling.

Once on the water, some of these lakes offer up surprises. Where else can you be within yards of a freeway in the middle of a city and relax to the song of redwing blackbirds and the croak of bullfrogs while muskrats swim around your canoe. And where was the local movie location for part of a Disney movie...just minutes from Greater Vancouver, no power boats and breathtaking scenery.

Buntzen Lake evening paddle. Jack Wainwright photo.

1. ALICE LAKE

•**Location:** on Highway 99, North of Squamish towards Whistler.

•**Description:** a small round lake with a Provincial Campsite at the north end. Picnicking, camping, swimming, hiking, fishing, no power boats allowed.

•**Access:** boat launch at provincial park, parking in lot provided.

This is a heavily used lake so it loses its wilderness appeal. Arrive early during peak season.

2. BURNABY LAKE

•**Location:** in the central valley of Burnaby, north of the freeway near Kensington off-ramp.

•**Description:** a three km long lake with very marshy shores. No power boats allowed except for the rowers and olympic paddler's pace boats.

•**Access:** paddlers will have to carry their canoe to the water's edge as there is no boat launch area. Three main access points are:

1. Burnaby Lake Pavillion south of Sprott St. off Sperling. Park in the paved lot with the rowers etc. Launch in the channel at the side of the Pavillion's access ramp. Stay off the wharf as it has been authorized for club use.

2. Still Creek: across the soccer fields on Sperling near C.G. Brown Pool. Park in the nearby lots. Check out the access before you carry your canoe as different water levels change the launching. Access to the lake has at times been blocked by a log.

3. Nature House at the foot of Piper St., south of Winston St.. Park in Nature House lot. This access is halfway down the lake. You can get different experiences depending on which direction you paddle.

This is not a heavily used area because it is marshy, however, it's a great bird watching site. Salmon once spawned in Still Creek, its main feeder and in Brunette R., its outflow connection to the Fraser R. As youngsters we caught crayfish there, but I haven't seen any there for years. Still creek is severely channeled now and in Vancouver much of it flows through long culverts. Brunette R. has a small dam on it maintaining the lake's water level. Nevertheless, this lake in the middle of Burnaby, offers a very relaxing wilderness experience. Muskrats frequent the west end, while evidence of beavers is visible at the east end. The freeway, just a few hundred meters away is a barely noticable background hum. Bullfrogs here are alien residents released from a failed frog farming enterprise. They went broke waiting the five years needed to mature bullfrogs. Mosquitoes can be a problem, be prepared.

3. BUNTZEN LAKE
•**Location:** At Anmore; take Ioco Rd. north from Port Moody and follows signs to Anmore and Buntzen.
•**Description:** This is a B.C. Hydro recreation area. It is a delightful few km of fjord-like wilderness. Fishing, hiking, swimming, no power boats, no alcohol.
•**Access:** At the end of the road at Anmore a prominent sign welcomes you to Buntzen, and warns that the gates are locked at night. Drive a km to the parking lots. Drive to the boat launch to unload at water's edge. Park in the large lots provided. Picnic tables and washrooms are only available at the south end near the parking lots and beach. Pit toilets are available at a small grassy beach at the far end. A hiking trail surrounds the lake. B.C. Hydro staff are always on site.

This lake was created in 1904 when the Vancouver Electric Company dammed the north end and built penstocks to power two generating stations at tide water on Indian Arm. A tunnel was driven through to Coquitlam Lake to provide additional water for generation. It can be seen by the grassy beach at the north end. It is tempting to canoe past the log barriers into the small lake above the still working penstocks. We used to paddle this part too, but irresponsible boaters venturing close to the outflow caused nervous hydro lawyers to have it blocked off.

This lake is a fantastic wilderness experience. A few years ago, as I paddled the far end, I spotted a small plane obviously crashed in the trees. As I drew nearer to investigate, a head appeared, told me to stay clear and explained that they were shooting a sequence for a Disney film.

Buntzen is a very popular lake on warm summer days and once the parking lots are full, traffic is halted at the gate. It is not a short portage from the gate to the lake, so arrive early. Most people stay at the south end and do not have boats, so the paddler still gets a wilderness experience even on a full use day.

We most often paddle to the far end exploring along the shore as we go, have lunch at the grassy beach, hike down the access road to a viewpoint above the generating plant on Indian Arm, and then paddle back along the other shore. This makes for a real stress-reducing break from the crush of urban life.

4. CULTUS LAKE
- **Location:** South of Chilliwack. Take exit #104 to #3 Rd. east of Abbotsford on Hwy 1 and follow the signs, or exit #119 at Cottonwood Corners Mall and follow Vedder Rd. south to Cultus Lake Provincial Park.
- **Description:** This lake is a gem about 5 km long and 1 km wide nestled in the Cascade Mountains. It is a low elevation lake and has been one of the most popular lower mainland lakeside retreats for over 60 years. The Provincial Park now takes up all the east side. Camp, hike, fish, paddle, swim.
- **Access:** Launch at the Park boat launch or carry to the side of a swimming beach.

The name Cultus means *bad* in Salish and was probably named for the deaths that occur there mostly because the winds funnelled by the mountains come up suddenly. Power boats, waterskiers and other powered water craft can also make this a hazardous experience for canoeists, especially in the high use summer months.

5. DEER LAKE (Burnaby)
•**Location:** In the central valley of Burnaby, south of Burnaby
Lake, off Burris, south on Buckingham, then 1/2 block north
on Sperling. The route is circuitous, but well-posted as this is a
popular beach.

•**Description:** This lake is a sheltered half mile long pothole
with marshy shores. No powerboats allowed. Fishing,
paddling, swimming, walking.

•**Access:** The only boat access is at the east end either over the
beach from the parking lot or near the boat rental concession.
This marshy muddy lake can give very relaxing paddling. The
shores, once surrounded by estates, a few private residences
and Oakalla Prison Farm are now mostly municipal park.
Walking trails have been built. The shores remain marshy and
home to various birds and amphibians. The lake has been
stocked for fishing, but it is not known for its fish. The geese
adopted the lake in great numbers, causing a high enough
coliform count at one time to ban swimming. The beach end
has washrooms and a food concession during the summer.

6. 7. DEER LAKE and HICKS LAKE (Harrison)
•**Location:** Northeast of Harrison Hot Springs in Sasquatch
Provincial Park.

•**Description:** These are more half mile long potholes, but
located in the forest east of Harrison. Camping, fishing,
electric motors only on Deer, 10 hp on Hicks. Three campsites.

•**Access:** Launch at the park boat launch ramps. Note: This is a
good area to see deer and bear.

8. HATZIC LAKE
•**Location:** North of Hwy. 7 between Hatzic and Dewdney.

•**Description:** This is another popular low elevation lake . Located
on the flat Fraser River flood plain, it may have been a river
channel thousands of years ago. Now it is surrounded by farms and
the large island which gives the lake its doughnut shape is covered
with resorts and homes. Speed restrictions of 8 & 50 km/h.

•**Access:** There is public access at the north end of Hatzic Island.

Unless you are staying at a resort here, you will find most other lakes are better suited to canoeing. The power boats and other powered watercraft at speeds up to 50km/h (30mph) and the narrow channels in places limit the enjoyment of paddling here.

If there is enough water at the bridge on Sylvester Rd., an alternate paddle is to the east up Chilqua Slough for a few kms. You can canoe through the first set of two large culverts, but the trip effectively ends at the next set. This slough is great for birdlife and lack of human intrusion. There is also a put-in at the bridge on Farms Rd., north of Hatzic which will let you canoe down Hatzic Slough into the lake if water levels permit. This slough is lined with homes.

9. HAYWARD LAKE
•**Location:** North of Ruskin off Hwy 7
•**Access:** Off Dewdney Trunk Road on the West side of the lake at Stave Falls or at the dam on the south end.
•**Description:** This lake was formed when the B.C. Electric Co. dammed Stave Lake for power. Three dams were built, two at the south end of Stave Lake and one part way down the Stave River creating Hayward Lake. The lakes were not logged prior to flooding and so still sport deadheads, rotted stumps and snags.

B.C. Hydro owns the surrounding land and has not yet developed its potential. As we were going to press, they informed us that they were improving the trail from the dam on Hayward Lake on the east side to the put-in at the north end. More landing sites, pit toilets and garbage cans are going in. Deadheads and floating debris will be cleaned up. There are no homes on Hayward Lake.

The Stave River below the dam can also be paddled, but signs warn of sudden surges of water from the dam. Access the Stave River just below the Hayward Lake Dam at the B.C. Hydro day-use area. From the Stave River put-in, it is possible to paddle into the Fraser where the closest take-out river right, would be at the park near the mouth of Kanaka Creek.

10. KAWKAWA LAKE

•**Location:** A few miles east of Hope, through town to 7th St.
then south to Kawkawa Lake Road.

•**Description:** This is another mile long, low elevation lake that
became popular years ago. It has a day use picnic site on the
southwest corner, otherwise private resorts and dwellings rule
the shore.

•**Access:** Either pay at a private resort or use the public boat
launch at the picnic site.

As this lake is well built on and there are no powerboat restrictions,
it is not the most desirable lake for relaxed paddling.

11. LAKE OF THE WOODS

•**Location:** A few miles north of Hope on Hwy. 1

•**Description:** This small round pothole surrounded as it is by
forest and mountains is a real gem. Fish, swim, paddle.

•**Access:** Park in the rest area lot and access the small beach via
a short steep path or pay at the resort at the north end.

This lake is a surprise as it is mostly wilderness and even though it
is on the highway, anyone in a canoe can find a private place to swim,
fish or just poke around exploring.

12. LOST LAGOON

•**Location:** Stanley Park entrance, Vancouver.

•**Description:** This was a tidal flat of Coal Harbour which was
dammed to create a lagoon.

•**Access:** None, as this is now a wildlife sanctuary.

This was a very popular rowing and paddling area 50 years ago
and the City of Vancouver even ran a boat rental concession there.
Now it is considered off-limits and a wildlife sanctuary. Vandalism to
habitat and the fountain probably contributed to the ban.

13. LIGHTNING LAKES

- **Location:** Manning Park, off Hwy. 3 east of Hope. Turn south just east of the lodge and follow signs to Lightning Lakes day use area.
- **Description:** A series of mountain lakes. No power boats allowed. Camp, fish, swim, hike, paddle.
- **Access:** At Manning Provincial Park's Lightning Lakes day-use area boat launch ramps.

These lakes have lots of shoreline to poke around exploring. Fishing can be excellent. Deer and bear are seen regularly. The powerboat ban adds considerably to the wilderness experience, even though these lakes are popular attractions. This is really a long way from the lower mainland for a day trip. It better lends itself to a weekend campover.

14. MILL LAKE

- **Location:** Clearbrook. Turn south off S. Fraser Way, onto Ware for one block, then west on Mill Lake Rd.
- **Access:** use the boat launch ramp at the end of Mill Lake Road. Park in the lot there.
- **Description:** This small peanut shaped lake is a high use recreational body of water for the Clearbrook Abbotsford area. Fish, paddle and bird-watch. No power boats.

This is the lake that Western Canoeing uses when people want to try out different models. It is fine for a picnic and a paddle if you are in the area, but there are better less-crowded waters in the area as noted in this section.

Evening on Mill Lake. Marlin Bayes photo.

15. MURRIN PARK (BROWNING LAKE)
- **Location:** A few km south of Squamish on Hwy. 99.
- **Description:** This little roadside lake is stocked for fishing, ok for swimming, and a bit limited for exploring, but interesting if it is not too crowded.
- **Access:** Portage from the Murrin Park parking lot. In spring look for the jelly blobs of amphibian eggs. Watch for the brown backs and orange bellies of western newts (salamanders).

16. ROLLEY LAKE
- **Location:** Rolley Lake Provincial Park, west of Stave Falls, about 4 km north of Dewdney Trunk Road on Bell St.
- **Description:** This small lake is only a km long but it is stocked for fishing, has a picnic area, swimming and hiking. No power boats.
- **Access:** No official boat launch, but portaging across the beach is easy.

This is another popular picnic area. The marshy shores are interesting to explore by canoe. Look for tree frogs in the spring, wood frogs in summer and western newts anytime.

17. SASAMAT LAKE
- **Location:** North of Ioco on the road to Belcarra Park.
- **Description:** A small low level lake about a km long. Swim, fish, paddle.
- **Access:** Bedwell Road parallels the lake on the west side. Park in White Pine Beach lot. Access via the paths to the beach.

This lake warms up nicely for swimming and is safe for novice paddlers, which is why the Association of Neighbourhood Houses operates Sasamat Outdoors Centre there.

18. TROUT LAKE

- **Location:** East Vancouver, John Hendry Park
- **Description:** This is a round pothole surrounded by peat bog.
- **Access:** None anymore. It is generally posted no boats, but the Vancouver Parks Board will give groups permits to use it.

The native bog brush and pines have all but disappeared as Vancouver Parks have attempted to improve it. There are still vestiges of the sphagnum moss that was reclaiming the area and the insect eating sun dew plants, too. Look for turtles that were once pets bought in stores and bullfrogs, that are also escaped aliens.

Sneaking up on a photo opportunity. Marlin Bayes photo.

Large Lakes

The large lakes within range of day trips from the greater Vancouver area are varied in size but all have one thing in common; they can be very dangerous for anyone paddling with no accompanying rescuers. The rule of thumb in our clubs is:
Three canoes make a safe trip.

Our large lakes are mostly steep-sided, fjord-like long fingers of water. The steep sides mean landing sites may be a mile apart or more and be just a tiny beach where a creek plummets down. These fjords tend to funnel and increase the velocity of the winds. It is difficult enough to make a self rescue in deep calm water on a nice day. It is almost impossible to make a self rescue in a squall. The water conditions that caused the capsize hinder the rescue. Add cold water in spring or fall and hypothermia lessens your strength and the time you have to save yourself. Most small boating deaths in B.C. are a result of these conditions. On the other hand, organized paddlers in B.C. have an almost unblemished record of no fatalities even though they encounter the same conditions. The ease with which another canoe can rescue a capsized one is what makes the difference.

That said, there is probably nowhere else in the world that offers such wilderness experiences so close to civilization. The steep slopes and small beaches have effectively limited road building and home building with the result that once you paddle off, you can be almost immediately into rugged country. In spring, snow avalanches still reach to the lake.

All manner of wildlife may be spotted on shore including mink, weasel, deer and bear. Camping is often possible although you have to find your own place and the thick undergrowth of our coastal rain forest limits tenting sites. Often too, the small beach you find will have a cabin near it, which doesn't help.

Unlike the USA, in Canada, ownership of waterfrontage legally ends at the historical high water mark which, by convention, means the zone where living woody vegetation begins. That usually means beaches are public domain. The exception to this may be where erosion has occured moving the shore within the surveyed boundaries of the land or where reservoirs have inundated plotted land. Of course it is best to ask permission to camp and not contest the fine legal points of ownership...especially if they have a big dog. Dogs do tend to regard trespassing on their perceived territory as acts of aggression. On the other hand our experience has been that people will go out of their way to accommodate paddlers. Perhaps they realize how vunerable we are to the elements or maybe they appreciate our reliance on paddle power and view us as kindred spirits. For whatever reason, we have encountered a lot of friendly folks back in the boondocks.

How far can you paddle comfortably on a day trip? All canoes are displacement type boats meaning their speed is determined by their hull shape and length. Cruising speed on water with no current is realistically about 4 km per hour. Poking in and out of bays adds considerably to the enjoyment and the length of the trip. A 16 km (10 mi.) round trip is all you should plan on. Most of our large lakes will require more than one day to get to the other end and return. Most lend themselves to weekend camping.

Exploring Harrison Lake. Marlin Bayes photo.

19. ALOUETTE LAKE
- **Location:** North of Haney. Take 232nd St. north to Fern St., follow Fern and the signs to Golden Ears Provincial Park.
- **Description:** This is an 18 km long lake that was enlarged when it was dammed at the south end to provide additional water for hydroelectric generators on Stave Lake. There are still some snags and deadheads but they do not interfer with paddlers.
- **Access:** Put in at the Park boat launch ramp or carry across the beach. Park in the lot.

As this is a popular recreation lake, a major hazard for paddlers is the waves generated by powerboaters. Parts of Alouette Lake are restricted to 8 km/hr. Most powerboaters, however, leave the shallows near shore to canoeists so we really can co-exist. Winds, limited landing sites and cold water hazards all exist on this lake. Exercise caution as noted in the introduction to our Large Lakes. Camping is permitted only in designated sites in the park. Golden Ears Park takes in all of the west side of Alouette Lake. A Correctional work camp is located on the east side across from the Park's public beaches.

According to birders, the name Golden Ears originated as a misunderstanding. Many years ago the mountain peaks there were home to Golden Eagles. They had built a nest or aerie that was reused continually for years. Bird Watchers referred to the area as the Golden Aeries. Non-birders heard it as the Golden Ears and perhaps because the peaks somewhat resemble ears and glow golden at sunset, the name stuck.

It is possible to portage over the ridge separating Alouette Lake and Stave Lake, however, it is a daunting trail as the ridge rises 300 m above the lakes. The Florence Lake Forestry Service Road in that area accesses Alouette Lake only through B.C. Correctional or B.C. Hydro property. There is no public access to or from that road and it does not permit access to Stave Lake except as noted on the map.

Poking in and out of bays adds considerably to the length of the trip. A paddle to the campsite at Gold Creek about five km up on the west side and return is a nice day trip.

20. CHILLIWACK LAKE
   •**Location:** South of Chilliwack at the end of the Chilliwack
      Lake Road.
   •**Description:** A wilderness lake just the right length for a day
      trip. It is in the large lake section because it has similar
      hazards of wind, cold water and remoteness.
   •**Access:** Put in at the boat launch at the north end. The road
      runs down the east side to the border so it is possible to take
      out at the far end if you can arrange a shuttle.

In the spring there are often several avalanches that will have
rumbled down as far as the lake. This lake is about 10 km long. It has a
Provincial Park with many campsites and a boat launch at the north
end and a beach once accessible by road at the south end. Fishing can
be excellent and is probably the main recreation on the lake. There are
no power restrictions. The road runs very close to the lake on the east
and thus detracts considerably from the wilderness vista. The most
scenic side to tour is the west, both coming and going. It is possible to
pole up the river and see the Canada - USA border clearings.

21. CHEHALIS LAKE
   •**Location:** North of Sasquatch Inn off Hwy. 7; near the
      bridge over the Harrison River.
   •**Description:** A wilderness lake of just the right length for a
      day trip. It is in the large lake section because it has similar
      hazards of wind, cold water and remoteness.
   •**Access:** Take the gravel road off the Morris Valley Rd. west of
      Sasquatch Inn for about 18 km. Unorganized parking.

This 10 km long lake has only become accessible due to logging
activities. It is a fairly high elevation for a coastal lake and is a
favourite fishing hole for many, especially after the lower lakes have
warmed up.

There are three forestry campsites on this lake. The first one has a
concrete boat launch. The second requires a portage to put in. A recent
DCC trip reported difficulty finding the lake due to a lack of
directional signs.

22. HARRISON LAKE
   •**Location:** Harrison Hot Springs.
   •**Description:** A huge lake 60 km long and up to 9 km wide.
      Lots of wilderness and every hazard mentioned in the large
      lake preamble.
   •**Access:** Portage over the beach at Harrison Hot Springs or
      follow the beach road east to a park and boat launch ramp. Park
      has washrooms.

A day trip is to circumnavigate Echo Island, the first large island in
the lake. As you go past the west side look for the two rock pinnacles
known as the Bear and the Owl. The associated legend speaks of days
long ago when everyone worked together for the common good except
two young men. One was from the Bear clan and the other was the
Owl totem. The Gods did not look kindly on their selfish behaviour
and when after several warnings they did not change their ways, the
Gods punished them by capsizing their canoe, changed them into stone
monuments of their totems and put them on this island as an example
to others.

Keep an eye on the wind and weather as any wind from the north
will make it very difficult to cross back to the launch site. One time we
had to wait well into evening before the wind dropped enough to allow
all our group to paddle back.

A four wheel drive dirt road follows the west side, but seldom
comes close enough to have an effect on paddlers. The west side has
the best and most frequent landing and camping sites. You should be
no more than 1 km (1/2) mile from a pull-out place anywhere on the
west side. The east side, especially after half way up, affords little
shelter for paddlers caught by the weather. Camping is unorganized.

Half way up on the west side of Harrison Lake there is a small bay
with a rock face. In the rock face is a natural window-like recess which
has a rock pinnacle shaped much like a welder's acetylene bottle. This
is the Witch Doctor! Here you must follow legend and practice by
sharing your lunch with the Witch Doctor as an offering to ensure safe
passage and calm waters. If you can't offer food, you may throw
money.

When we checked out this lake, we did so by power boat. When we left Harrison Hot Springs, it was dead calm. At the Doctor there was a two foot chop. At Port Douglas at the north end, it was again calm. It was the same when we returned. The reason may have been the lower terrain at the Doctor which allowed east-west winds to roil the water. In any case, you won't want to take chances by ignoring the Witch Doctor.

This lake, serviced by paddlewheelers, was the route of choice to the gold fields through Lillooet and on to the Cariboo, before the Royal Engineers pushed through the Fraser Canyon wagon road.

This is not a lake to take chances on. Away from the populated south end, there are few people. It is a wide lake and power boaters can easily miss seeing a capsized canoe. Stay reasonably close to shore and keep your weather eye open. Do not paddle this lake without another boat for rescue. Three canoes make a safe trip.

23. PITT LAKE

- •**Location:** North of Haney.
- •**Description:** This is a 28 km tidal lake. Fjord-like with rugged shores and a big mud flat.
- •**Access:** Take Dewdney Trunk Road to Neaves Rd., north on Neaves to the boat launch area on Pitt River at the end of this road. Or north on Harris, east on McNeil, north on Neaves.

The ocean tides affect the Fraser River as far up as Mission. Pitt Lake experiences tidal action up to 2.6 m (8 ft.). Some say it is the only tidal lake in the world, but I find that hard to believe. This lake has not been dammed, so the shoreline is quite natural but steep.

This was a saltwater fjord after the last ice age 12,000 years ago. The ice piled higher than the surrounding mountains, scouring them rounded as it flowed. B.C. was not covered by an ice sheet, but by alpine glaciers which merged and flowed down the valleys. Look around and you can see mountains that must have poked through the ice, because they have not been rounded as much as the lower level ones have. Our land here is still rising after being depressed by the glaciers, thus this lake is now fresh water, but still low enough to experience tides.

The put-in is at the boat launch ramp on Pitt River near where it out flows the lake. There are channel markers which must be noted and used by everyone. There is a huge tidal mud flat exposed at low tide on the west side of the lake near the south end. Several small boaters have lost their lives over the years here when a falling tide stranded them in the mud and squalls capsized them. This shallow shelf generates breaking waves when the rest of the lake is just choppy.

Winds can always come up suddenly in these fjords. In Pitt Lake they can be especially dangerous. We explored the area by small power boat, researching this book. A wind started to blow up the Pitt River and before we knew it, we were in four foot waves! We ran with the wind to the lee of an island half way down the lake. There we secured everything and started back. Our 65 hp outboard had to be cut back to the point where we were barely making headway. Every few waves one would wash right over us.

People on shore later told us that they thought we had sunk because they had lost sight of us in the troughs. Had we been in a canoe, we would have headed for shore right away and waited out the wind. Had we been on the mud flat in a canoe, there would have been no survivors.

Nevertheless, this is not a bad place for canoeing. Fish, swim, paddle. No restrictions on power boats. Camping is unorganized. Try the far end, sites can be found near the logging road there.

Headless Valley is rugged remote country at the head waters of the Pitt. Legends tell of a lost gold mine there and the finding of a decapitated body. Perhaps the Sasquatch lives there too.

Dodging the Stave Lake stumps. Doug Brunt photo.

24. STAVE LAKE

   •**Location:** North of Ruskin at Stave Falls.
   •**Description:** A 28 km reservoir, fjord-like, deadheads and
      snags.
   •**Access:** Put in at the boat launch on the west arm off Florence
      Lake Forest Service Road above the dam or 10 km farther up
      on the west side or halfway up the lake at Cypress Point on the
      east side.
      To get to Cypress Point take Sylvester Road north from Hwy.
      7. Where the road starts to climb, it is 21.5 km of decent
      gravel road to the put-in at the B.C. Forest Service campsite at
      the mouth of Salisbury Creek. Keep to the main road, pass
      Davis Lake on your left. At 10 km sign go left at the Y. Stay
      on main road for next 11.5 km. Obey signs for Cypress Point.
      The end of the lake is a 12 km paddle from here.

The dam and generators are located at the south end of the west
arm. They are protected by a boom of logs. Avoid the area. There is
plenty of good paddling up this long lake. In the days when
hydro-electric development raised the lake level, there was no thought
given to clear cutting the area first. Timber was plentiful and clearing
this remote region would not have been economically sound. Besides,
recreation was a rich man's pursuit and there were lots of other lakes
around. The drowned trees have long since rotted leaving stumps
above and below the waterline. Actually, in some places they make
excellent slalom courses for paddlers wanting to sharpen their paddling
skills. However when the wind comes up, they are a significant hazard
for paddlers. There are ongoing efforts to remove these hazards by
B.C. Corrections crews and B.C. Hydro.

Fish, swim and explore in this lake. Camping is unorganized. A
good site is up the river which is paddleable until the first drop. Just
past there is a good gravel beach with sandy tent sites. Summer camps
for children are run on this lake.

Stave Lake got its name from the barrel staves cut there in the 19th
century. The barrels were no doubt commissioned by The Hudson Bay
Co. at Fort Langley to ship out the abundant salmon, which along with
spars and furs, were early exports.

Saltwater Day Trips

A very interesting aspect to paddling in the Canadian southwest is the saltwater/tidal trips possible. Our fjords are only duplicated in a few places in the world and on a clear day the scenery is breathtaking. Tides add another dimension. Our coastal rise and fall generally occurs twice daily with differences of up to 4 m. Canoes, being so portable, are not limited to the same extent as powerboats. If the tide is out, we just carry the craft a little farther. On the other hand, the cautions of fjord canoeing apply. The winds can come up suddenly and landing sites are limited. An additional hazard is powerboat waves. Commercial marine traffic generates good sized swells. These merge and rebound off the shore creating interesting challenges for paddlers even on windless days.

Saltwater speeds corrosion but its effect on canoes is negligible. About the only material at risk is aluminum and only then if you have used other metals for accessories. If you are concerned, just hose it down after the trip. Certainly don't use that as an excuse to avoid the fun of saltwater trips.

25. BURRARD INLET (EAST)
- **Location:** North of Burnaby and Port Moody.
- **Description:** 14.5 km (9 miles) long and up to 2 km (1.5 miles) wide. Not very fjord-like. Hazards are lots of powerboaters and some commercial freighters and tankers. A big tidal mud flat is exposed at low tide at the far east end.
- **Access:** Use the boat launches at Rocky Point (Port Moody) and Cates Park (North Vancouver). Or portage over the beaches at public accesses at mouth of Seymour River (N. Van), Old Orchard Park (across from Port Moody) or Barnet Marine Park (Burnaby).

This area is very interesting to paddle. Along the Burnaby shore are refineries and a railroad interspersed with barnacled beaches and old pilings. Port Moody has a large bulk sulphur loading facility and sawmill.

The east end is a tidal mudflat where the rising tide can cover the beach faster than you can run trying to avoid it. When the tide is high here, the water meets the evergreens transforming the area into a calendar picture on a calm day. The north shore still holds the remains of once thriving sawmills and shingle mills.

Walk around Old Orchard Park and discover the orchard that I used to play in fifty years ago and it was abandoned then. Next paddle past waterfront homes that may have got their start as summer cabins and on to the refinery at Ioco (named for the Imperial Oil Co.) Next to Ioco is the B.C. Hydro thermal generating plant.

The rest of the north shore was a federal military reserve and may now be park reserve but it is still rugged forest and small white shell beaches right around to Belcarra Park. Cross the North Arm channel with care as currents converge there and depending on the tide, a canoeist can encounter severe turbulence.

As you cannot circumnavigate this whole area in one reasonable day, a better plan would be to avoid the North Arm crossing and put in on the North Vancouver side. Cates Park is a wilderness area and west of that is Indian reserve with tidal flats and the hulks of old boats. Near the Second Narrows Bridge, Hooker Chemical Works turns salt from the southern US and Mexico into chemicals for our pulp and paper industry. A shipyard marks the mouth of the Seymour River.

Strong currents flow under the bridge through Second Narrows. Many a freighter has had difficulty there. It is no place for a canoe! It is also a legal requirement that watercraft be under power at both the First and Second Narrows bridges. Although the currents are weaker away from the bridge, the frequent powerboats and commercial marine traffic make it inadvisable for a slow canoe to cut across their channels. A canoe is virtually invisible on radar and in a channel of this nature the powered boats have limited maneuverability.

26. BURRARD INLET (WEST)

- **Location:** North of Vancouver.
- **Description:** This is a bustling international seaport almost all commercially developed with few official recreational areas. It is about 10 km long.
- **Access:** No official access. South side: portage over the Stanley Park seawall or over rough riprap along Commissioner St. near New Brighton Park close to the   Second Narrows. Portside Park accessed off the north end of Main Street has a good beach for launching, but no parking except at the pay lot next to the Sea Bus terminal 500 m farther west. ($6 for all day). North shore access is worse. Try the foot of Pemberton. Launch over coarse riprap to a gravel beach exposed only at low tide. Parking there appears informal and unposted.

With all the commercial traffic, canoes really have no business being here. But it is interesting to put in at Stanley Park and explore Coal Harbour (the marina is private and guarded and you will be challenged if you explore there). Paddle by the Bayshore Hotel staying out of the way of the racing shells. Paddle by Canada Place with its seven sails, the Cruise Ship docks, a replica of the Beaver (first steamer on the coast) and past various wharves and grain elevators all with their deepsea vessels totally dwarfing you. Then you can either go on to Brighton Park to take out and shuttle back for the car or paddle back. Starting at Portside Park lets you go each way from the middle.

The north shore is less interesting in its variety, and difficult to access for a day's paddle. The foot of Pemberton is the best of a bunch of poor choices. It is possible to put in under the bridges, but the current is so strong at certain tides that it is not worth the risk. And it is illegal. Only powered craft may use the waters of the First and Second Narrows. The combination of powered marine traffic, narrow channels, strong currents and rebounding waves is more than anyone should challenge in a canoe.

The general marine traffic rule that sail (and paddles) have the right of way over power has exceptions. Powered marine traffic often has the right of way in narrow channels. Canoes interferring could face court charges.

27. ENGLISH BAY
- **Location:** South of West Vancouver.
- **Description:** A wide (4 to 5 miles) body of water with about 10 km of shore on the north side, 5 km along Stanley Park, 7 km along the south shore with another 7 km around to the Fraser River. The area is mostly beaches, bluffs and residences with a sprinkling of commercial activities.
- **Access:** North Shore: access at Ambleside Park or Dundarave Beach. If you have to take out in an emergency, you will find other minor accesses as public or private trails from the many small beaches.

  Stanley Park: put in at Third Beach

  South Shore: put in at Sunset Beach, Vanier Park boat launch, Maritime Museum, Kitsilano Beach, Jericho Beach, Locarno Beach or Spanish Banks.

At the mouth of the Fraser, which strictly speaking is not English Bay, you can put in at Iona Island recreation area or at MacMillan boat launch ramp on Sea Island.

Deep sea shipping lanes traverse English Bay. The ships move quite quickly and can create huge swells. Several ships on the move can create hazardous standing waves that merge and rebound off rocky headlands. Canoeing a bit offshore minimizes these, but landing can be tricky. One of our club members, prior to landing, decided to take off his shoes so he would not get them wet in the surf. As he put his head down, a rebounding wave pitched him right out of the canoe.

A nice trip can be from Ambleside Park to Point Atkinson and return. Avoid paddling across the shipping lanes to Stanley Park. Instead, put in at third beach and explore both ways along the shore. Avoid Lions Gate Bridge waters.

There are no serious problems paddling anywhere on the south shore between Stanley Park and Spanish Banks. Powerboaters launch and use False Creek but they are restricted to 8 km/hr. Take out almost anywhere in an emergency. Spanish Banks has a half-mile of sandbank at low tide and the shallows there can quickly generate breaking waves.

From Spanish Banks around Point Grey's bluffs to the mouth of the Fraser, there is beach, but no convenient road access to haul a canoe out. The mouth of the Fraser can be extremely dangerous in certain tide and wind configurations. Powerboaters have problems then and it is certain that paddlers will too.

English Bay has a legacy from WW II. At Jericho a large concrete ramp and hangars serviced "Flying Boats" or amphibious planes. Gun emplacements and searchlight platforms can still be seen at Narrows North under the Lions Gate Bridge, at Ferguson Point near Third Beach and at Point Grey at the bottom of the bluffs. The only serious shot fired was one that splintered the wheelhouse of a yacht that refused to identify itself. Turns out it was piloted by an American naval officer who thought he was exempt from reporting.

English Bay offers a unique experience. Doug Brunt photo.

28. FALSE CREEK

- **Location:** South of downtown Vancouver.
- **Description:** A 3.3 km finger of tidewater bordering the southern boundary of the peninsula of downtown Vancouver. Hazards are few but there is lots of traffic. Speed is limited to 8 km/h.
- **Access:** Put in and park at Sunset Beach, the Maritime Museum or Vanier Park boat launch ramp.

This is an interesting short trip. The south shore skirts Granville Island Public Market and all the related shops. This area was highly industrialized with steel mills, ship yards, saw mills and even a cooperage. Now there are just remnants of industry as the area is rebuilding as residential with ancillary services such as Science World and marinas. Expo 86 occupied most of the north shore replacing the industries almost overnight and is now becoming a mix of residential and business activities. A public walkway will soon extend all around False Creek.

29. INDIAN ARM (NORTH ARM OF BURRARD INLET)

- **Location:** North of Deep Cove and Belcarra Park.
- **Description:** This is an 18 km long coastal fjord with limited canoe landing sites. Hazards include winds and power boats.
- **Access:** On the west side put in at the Cates Park boat launch ramp or carry to the beach from the Deep Cove beach parking lot. On the east side carry to the beach at Belcarra Park or Bedwell Bay.

Between Cates Park and Belcarra Park on the other side there are some very strong currents. Paddlers should avoid them by staying reasonably close to shore and not attempting a crossing until the channel widens off Deep Cove.

A pleasant paddle is to put in at Deep Cove, paddle across to Jug Island and explore the shore around Bedwell Bay. Bedwell Bay has interesting tidal mud, sand and rock flats exposed at low tide. Clam digging and crabbing was good here, but pollution has contaminated them now. The Vancouver Water Ski Club has a course and clubhouse here.

Up the east shore of Indian Arm, named for Indian River which empties into this fjord at the north end, you pass the Buntzen power houses. These were constructed in 1904 by the Vancouver Electric Company to provide power to the young city and its street cars. Twin Islands house a marine park where you can camp overnight or picnic.

On high-use days only early birds will get in. This is as far as you will probably go on a day trip. This circuit, from Deep Cove and return, can be done as a late afternoon and evening paddle.

The rest of the east shore to Indian River is steep forested shores with cabins or the remains of dwellings on most landing sites. Granite Falls near Indian River was a large abandoned area with lots of potential camping sites, but at the time we checked it out, it was posted *No trespassing*.

As this book was going to press, the Greater Vancouver Regional District announced the purchase of Granite Falls and Crocker Island for use as a future GVRD park.

Indian River is an active logging zone, with the logs being delivered to the tidewater booming grounds there. It is possible to paddle and pole up the river at least to the logging road as we did. A few tent sites can be hacked out there. The fresh water of the river layers over the saltwater of Indian Arm creating an interesting differential.

Look for seals and otters. Killer whales visit infrequently. Fishing can be good and the lack of industry has minimized the problem of pollution and contaminated fish as found in Howe Sound fjord and Burrard Inlet.

Returning down the west shore you find Wigwam Inn. This resort has gone through many transformations in its history since the 1920's.

The Harbour Navigation boats serviced the many summer homes along the way to Wigwam Inn and provided day trips for foot passengers who ate at the Inn, hiked to the Spray of Pearls Falls and then sailed back to Vancouver on the return trip of the Scenic. The Scenic now does charters out of Vancouver or Steveston when the Sea Lions are there. For a while the Inn had a shadowy existance with gambling being suggested as a way to survive. Wigwam Inn catered to the many power boaters who chugged there for evening meals or day trip excursions. Now, we understand it is owned by the Royal Vancouver Yacht Club and is restricted to members only.

The west shore is steeply forested with canoe landing sites every 1.5 km or so. These are often no more than small alluvial fans, with very limited tenting sites. An exception is the overgrown abandoned site of unknown origin...probably a floating logging camp that had some facilities on shore. It is interesting to note that this whole fjord had been logged back in the days of hand logging which meant taking the best and ignoring the rest. Look for this site a few miles south of Wigwam Inn on your right in the Crocker Island Channel.

About halfway back you will pass Silver Falls as they cascade into the ocean. You can even paddle your canoe close enough to get the spray. Silver Falls is the limit for anyone daytripping out of Deep Cove.

As you paddle closer to Deep Cove, summer camps and private homes become thicker, and add an interesting diversion from the quiet forest.

It is important that you watch the weather as squalls can come up suddenly. Do not travel without other canoes along to help with possible rescues. Note that landing sites are not frequent. Power boats are often numerous and can generate waves but they tend to stay offshore and watch where they are going so they are not much of a hazard. They also may not see a canoe that upsets close to shore. There is no industry or commercial marine traffic to worry about on this inlet.

Exploring Indian Arm in a Clipper Sea-1. Doug Brunt photo.

30. 31. HOWE SOUND

- **Location:** West of and between West Vancouver and Squamish.
- **Description:** A fjord 48 km (30 miles) long by about 12 km (7.5 mi.) wide.
- **Access:** Use the boat launches available at many sites along the east shore : Horseshoe Bay, Sunset Marina, Lions Bay, Porteau Cove, Squamish. On the west side use Gibsons and Port Mellon.

This is a typical fjord, but because it is so close to Metro Vancouver, it is busy with boaters, ferries, and some freighters. Almost all the flat land is built upon. Finding wilderness campsites is all but impossible. Public campsites are available on Keats Island and at Porteau Cove.

The pulp and paper mills on the west side, the heavy industry at Squamish and the now closed copper mine at Britannia have contributed to the pollution of this fjord. The area is now closed to commercial harvesting of ground fish, crabs and clams. It is safe to eat the salmon as they only migrate through. Forty years ago this area was the fisherman's paradise for Greater Vancouver.

A day trip is to put in at Horseshoe Bay and paddle to Gibsons and back, exploring the north end of Bowen Is. and Keats along the way. This is a ferry route so stay close to shore. Watch the weather for winds and squalls from the north. Do not paddle this area without rescue capacity ie. three canoes make a safe trip. Gambier Island's south side with its three major bays can be explored as an alternative.

To give more time to explore Keats and the Paisley Islets, take the Bowen Island Ferry, drive to Tunstall Bay on the other side and put in there. This also gets you away from a lot of the hazardous traffic.

Putting in at Porteau or Brittania Beach will let you paddle the north half to Squamish. BC Rail follows the shore on the east, while the highway tends to move inland. The west side is steep with few landing places. The winds can be very strong and sudden in this part of Howe Sound. Do not paddle here without rescue capacity.

Currents are not a major concern for the paddler in Howe Sound, but ferry traffic is. Between Bowen Is. and West Vancouver, the

Ferries from Vancouver Is. pass every hour. They move at upwards of 22 knots and can generate good waves. There is also a ferry to Bowen Is. in this area and a ferry to Gibsons north of Bowen. If a ferry comes close to a paddler, there is little chance to avoid serious problems.

Paddlers must realize that they are virtually invisible on radar. On crossing any channel, paddlers must stay close together to maximize visibility and block as little of the channel as possible. Otherwise, paddle reasonably close to shore for a peaceful day.

Watch for ferry traffic in Howe Sound. Doug Brunt photo.

Easy River Day Tripping

The following lower mainland rivers are very forgiving of novice paddlers. The currents are generally slow and there are few hazards. Should a dumping occur, there is ample opportunity to reach shore safely.

River paddling generally calls for a shuttle as it is usually too difficult to paddle back upstream. Following the rule that three canoes make a safe trip, you will probably have more than one vehicle. You can either leave a vehicle at the take-out by doubling up passengers and gear or dump all the gear at the put-in and run a car back to the take-out. Every paddler should have a plan that will allow him to shuttle an extra canoe. For instance, roof racks can be temporarily extended with 2x3s duct taped to the short ones or a second canoe can be angled on the short racks. On vans and other vehicles where the roof will take the weight, a third canoe can be secured on 2x3s that have been drilled to take ropes to tie them to the racks and top canoe.

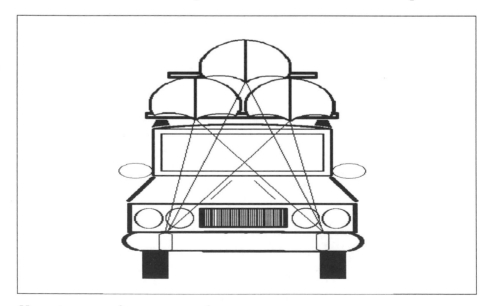

How to carry three or more boats at once.

32. HARRISON RIVER

- **Location:** between Harrison Lake and the Fraser River.
- **Description:** A 17 km (10.5 miles) long, fairly wide, slow current river. Hazards are few. Wind can be a problem.
- **Access:** Put in at the south beach on Harrison Lake. Leave vehicles parked away from the beach area. Take out at Kilby Park on Harrison Bay, south of the Hwy. 7 bridge over Harrison River (Follow the signs to Kilby Store Museum).

This is a short trip, so there is lots of time to explore along the way, swim and have a leisurely lunch too. At the put-in, it is suggested that you relocate your vehicle to one of the back roads as a courtesy to others who wish to use the beach.

As you paddle off, stay to the left (west) shore of Harrison Lake. The river will be apparent on your left in 10 minutes or so. Along the way you will pass the concrete tanks that are the Hot Springs water storage. The springs themselves are under the lake and were discovered by people who capsized in winter and found themselves in warm water. The heat source is part of the Mount Baker thermal pool.

This river is generally forested with steep shores. There is almost no development on it except where Weaver Creek Road extends to the north shore and there a few homes are found. Along the way on the south bank (river left) you will find the wreck of a steam engine. Was it from a boat or a logging donkey engine? An Indian cemetery is next. The Native People do not appreciate trespassers here. A beach and remains of a house hidden on a bench of flat land make a good lunch break. Was this place someone's dream home or an artifact from our logging history? Huntley's Cabin beach on a spit of land above Hwy. 7 is a good place for a swim. It is private only to the high water mark, but ask permission if Huntley is there. He is another Dogwood Canoe Club member.

On the north shore (river right) as you leave Harrison Lake, there are booming tie up piles and there may be booms. The river has some shallows here. The channel is more center and south. Next come the few homes at the end of Weaver Creek Road. Morris Slough is a 5 km diversionary side trip up Weaver Creek. The Weaver Creek Spawning Channel can be reached by paddle power. In the fall, spawning salmon fill the channel. You are not allowed to canoe in the spawning channel of course. There is also a $500 fine for molesting spawning salmon anywhere so be careful when canoeing up Morris Slough and Weaver Creek in spawning season. Poles and paddles pushing into the gravel disturb wild spawning areas, so proceed cautiously. In this area you can find a swimming hole and a good lunch break site. You may also be host to not a few mosquitoes! At the entrance to Morris Slough there is a bluff with limited canoe landing space, but well worth the stop and the climb for the view. The DCC calls this Ivy's Bump. This also makes a good lunch stop and the bluff usually has a breeze that keeps down the mosquitoes.

As you near the Hwy. 7 bridge there are gravel shoals and islands near the middle and left of the river. The current quickens considerably along the pilings on river right. Pass under the center span of the Hwy. 7 bridge. Take-out can be either just past the bridge at river right, at a road end on river left or paddle on down to Kilby Park on river left where there is a good beach and parking area.

Headwinds can often be a problem for the last half of this trip. However, the current on this river is slow enough that if headwinds are too strong, it is quite possible to turn around and paddle back to the put-in.

Rest stop on the Harrison. Marlin Bayes photo.

33. HOPE SLOUGH

•**Location:** Chilliwack.

•**Description:** This is a unique urban paddling experience on lake grade water 16 km. (10 mi.) one way.

•**Access:** Put in at the McGrath Road Bridge just north of Yale Road or another 7 km west on Yale Rd. at Reeves Rd.. Take out at Berkley and Cawley just west of Young Rd. The take-out is a 50 m carry as the access road to the park has been blocked by curbing.

This may have been an old meander of the Fraser, but now it is a lake grade slough that wends past nicely kept homes, wild swampy shores and a country club. Considering that Hope Slough goes through urban areas, it is now surprisingly litter-free and a credit to Chilliwack. When we paddled it years ago, we got enough returnable bottles to pay for the trip! Still, it is a unique area to paddle. Watch for frogs and salamanders.

This trip may be done with a shuttle or put in at the Berkley access and paddle up and back. As a shuttle, on this still water, 16 km. is a day's paddling. As a return trip plan on only getting to the Reeves Bridge and back.

34. FRASER RIVER (Hope to Rosedale)

•**Location:** Hope B.C.

•**Description:** 38 km (24 miles) of big volume grade one water

•**Access:** Put in on the Coquihalla River in Hope or under the Hope end of the bridge over the Fraser. Take out at Ferry Park river left just past the Rosedale Bridge .

Watch for boils and waves rebounding off the shore. There is a log trap about 10 km downstream of Hope which requires you to stay on river left to go through the gate. Do not paddle the Fraser in high water. This trip requires a shuttle and is a long drive from Vancouver, but it is a very relaxing trip. Picnic on the gravel bars and drift along. If you paddle all out, the trip will be over before you know it. Racers do it in two hours, but you won't.

35. FRASER RIVER (Rosedale to Vancouver)

•**Location:** Between the Rosedale-Agassiz Bridge and
MacDonald boat launch ramp on Sea Island.

•**Description:** 130 km (82 mi.) of big volume river. Hazards
include boils, fast currents, commercial and recreational
marine traffic. All hazards are avoidable, thus this is considered
an easy river. A shuttle is required.

•**Access:** See the map for more accurate access details.
Put in at Ferry Park under the south end of the
Rosedale-Agassiz Bridge. Take out near Dewdney on
Nicomen Island or at the Dewdney Regional Park.

Ferry Park to Dewdney Regional Park is a 38 km (24 mi.) day trip.
Or take out river left at the beach just past the Mission Bridge another
14 km (9 mi.) or 10 km (6 mi.) past Mission Bridge, river left of
Crescent Is. at River Road or another 12 km (7.5 mi.) at Fort Langley
Park, river left of McMillan Island or another 6 km (3.75 mi.) river left
to Derby Reach Regional Park.

Dewdney Regional Park to Derby Reach is a 42 km (26.25 mi.)
day trip or another 8 km (5 mi.) at Barnston Is. Ferry, river left of
Barnston Is. or another 8 km (5 mi.) under Port Mann Bridge, river
right, boat launch ramp or another 16 km (10 mi.) river right at
Burnaby's Fraser Foreshore Park.

Derby Reach to Fraser Foreshore Park is a 32 km (20 mi.) day
trip. or another 12 km (7.5 mi.) river left at MacDonald boat launch
ramp on Sea Is. Port Mann boat launch to MacDonald boat launch is a
28 km (17.5 mi.) day trip.

Port Mann boat launch to the Annacis Island bridge access is 11
km (6.8mi.) or another 13 km (8 mi.) to Deas Is. Regional Park for a
24 km (15 mi.) day trip.

As this river has a decent current, you can easily, lazily paddle 40
km in a day. The current slows near the mouth so the day trips are
shorter. If you really go all out, you can do this trip in one day, but
you won't have time to smell the flowers! Camping out is possible at
the GVRD parks along the way. Vehicle access and parking are good
at each named access. Other accesses are available between Rosedale
and Port Mann, but below Port Mann Bridge, industry and private

ventures severely limit where you can get off the river. River right at Byrne road in Burnaby is a good access for a lunch break if you take a day trip from Port Mann to MacDonald take-out.

The hazards on this part of the Fraser River are easily avoided. Watch for boils where the water moves vertically creating a hump that causes your canoe to slide off sideways. This is always disconcerting to novice paddlers. Control the action by bracing your paddle and going with the flow. Never fight the current.

At certain water levels the confluence of the Harrison River with the Fraser can be a challenge. In higher water there are often serious standing waves river right and a whirlpool river left. The best route in high water is to run down the centre.

Where the river braids, canoeists must make route choices. If in doubt, always take the one with the most water flowing. In other words, go with the flow.

Use extreme caution when paddling the saltwater shores of the mouth of the Fraser. The huge mudflats can trap you on a falling tide and there is no walking to shore!

The Fraser River is tidal as far up as Mission thus the current will be faster on a falling and low tide than on a rising tide. Where the Fraser meets Georgia Strait at both the North Arm, the Middle Arm and the South Arm, the combination of wind, tide and current spells problems for paddlers. Do not paddle downstream of Steveston unless you are very experienced. The strong current along the jetty makes returning difficult.

To daytrip the south arm, which is the one the freighters use, put in from Annacis Is. off Pembina St. and take out river left at Deas Island Regional Park, at Canoe Pass near Westham Is. or river right at Steveston. Stay left on this arm to explore several natural islands of the Fraser delta. Picnic there along the way. The currents away from the main flow are gentle and easily paddled against if you wish to avoid a shuttle. If you do make a circuit, consider starting by paddling upstream and then you have the current to return on.

The middle arm of the Fraser divides Sea Island from Lulu Island (Richmond) It is not recommended as there are marinas with lots of powerboaters, float planes landing at the airport and poor accesses.

Seals are regularly seen in the lower Fraser. Sea Lions migrate, but when the salmon are running, they use the Steveston jetty as home and range up the Fraser at least through all its tidal length. Because of the potentially dangerous water conditions, the sea lions on the jetty are best seen by taking a commercial tour. Try Hope to Port Mann as a weekend or three day camping trip. There is unorganized camping on the islands, river bars and secluded beaches. Go in medium to low water levels.

36. NICOMEKL RIVER
•**Location:** Between Langley and Crescent Beach.
•**Description:** 15 km (9 mi.) of gentle river. Few hazards.
•**Access:** Put in at the south end of the bridge on 203 St. near
51st Ave. (West of Portage Park). Park in the lot just north of
the bridge. Take out south of 99A Highway.

The Nicomekl was the canoe route chosen to found a Hudson Bay post that would not be in the USA at about the time the BNA Act was drawing the border between Canada and the States. In 1824 James McMillan went up the Nicomekl, portaged at Langley (now Portage Park at 204 St.) over to the Salmon R. at about 72nd Ave. and Glover and down to the Fraser where he chose the site for Fort Langley. Portage Park had a cairn with a plaque commemorating the route. The plaque is now gone although you can still find the cairn at a bend in the river in the park. We don't paddle from the park as there is no reasonable access and the river is hazardous with shopping buggy deadheads.

This river has been channeled somewhat at the start and now has a walking trail alongside the first part. The dikes hem one's view to the extent that you feel like you are paddling in a ditch. The dike banks are grassy, have wild flowers and grazing cattle.

The current is usually slow enough to be able to paddle back upstream and avoid a shuttle. **If you are avoiding a shuttle, always start by paddling upstream so you have the current to return on.**

37. NICOMEN SLOUGH
- **Location:** Hwy. 7, east of Mission.
- **Description:** 15 km (9 mi.) of lake grade water. No shuttle required. Few hazards.
- **Access:** Park off the road at the south end of the Hwy 7 bridge at Deroche. Put in over the grassy bank there.

Nicomen Slough is an old meander of the Fraser River. Paddling east eventually gets you to a virtually impassable swamp. It may be passable in high water by spry paddlers who enjoy hopping out to haul over logs and push their way through thick beds of reeds. According to the map, it should get you into the Fraser whereupon you can paddle downstream and make a circle route of it. We quit before we got that far.

Paddling west from the put-in is like paddling on a long thin lake. If you go far enough, you will end up in the Fraser River. The banks are relatively low and run through farm lands. The only hazard we encountered on this part was real soft boot grabbin' mud at one place when we lunched and explored at the mouth of Norrish Creek.

This is a great place to see waterfowl anytime. As well, a flock of Trumpeter Swans has wintered here for many years.

38. PITT RIVER AND WIDGEON CREEK
- **Location:** North of Pitt Meadows.
- **Description:** The Pitt River is a wide, tidal 19 km (12 mi.) river that flows into the Fraser.
- **Access:** Put in at the boat launch ramp at the north end of 208 Street (Neaves Rd./ Rannie Rd.). Take out 3 km down the Fraser just past the Port Mann bridge, river right at the boat launch ramp. Or cut the trip short by paddling up the Alouette R. and take out at the bridge on Harris Rd.

The Pitt R. has very muddy banks and varied speed due to tidal action. It is shallow therefore winds can create some big waves. The two bridges are not a concern, stay in the middle. There is no significant hazard on entering the Fraser. The worst hazard on this river may be the powerboats. Water skiers play on it and on the

Alouette River too.

An easy daytrip from the Pitt boat launch ramp is to go directly across the river to WIDGEON CREEK. This is a short, pleasant paddle and is one we often start our paddling season with. It can be crowded in summer, but you may have it all to yourself in early spring. Paddle as far as you can up the creek, pull out on the sandy beach have lunch there and if you are feeling energetic, hike the few miles up the road to the falls. A shuttle is not needed for Widgeon Creek.

36. PITT POLDER
  •**Location:** As above for the Pitt River.
  •**Description:** Rather than a river, this is a series of channels
      that drain this once marshy area.
  •**Access:** Put in at the open slough to the right of the dike east of
      the boat launch and paddle east.

This area was drained by Dutch settlers (Netherlands Community Agricultural Reclamation Area). These channels may be interconnected, but the challenge is to find the route. Most trips end up portaging across dikes to the next channel. The bird life is fascinating. You can see all sorts of raptors (hawks, eagles...) Trumpeter swans winter here. Sand Hill Cranes and Herons nest nearby.

After launching, there should be only one dike between you and the lake. Paddle across the slough towards the mountain on the far side. In the far corner, portage over the southern dike into the ditch. Paddle west to a large channel and follow it south. This divides into several channels...take your choice. If when returning you turn left at the large channel, you should get back to start without a portage. Good luck in the maze...heh, heh, heh!

40. RIVER OF GOLDEN DREAMS
  •**Location:** near Whistler B.C.
  •**Description:** A picturesque narrow slow moving stream
      between Alta Lake and Green Lake. A shuttle is required and
      the trip will take all day.
  •**Access:** Put in at Alta Lake. Take out at Green Lake.
The lakes have waterfowl, waterlilies and other wildlife. Bears

have been seen when the berries are ripe. The river offers a chance to practice river skills like ferrying and reading the water. Dumpings have occurred when inexperienced paddlers miscalculated but the river is not dangerous so it is a good one for people learning river skills. This is not a "float" trip. You will have to maneuver.

41. SALMON RIVER
- **Location:** North of Langley.
- **Description**: This is a slow narrow stream. Downstream of Rawlinson Road the river meanders to the Fraser. The total trip is about 12 km (7.5 mi.).
- **Access:** You can put in at 72nd Ave. and Springbrook Rd. but you will be faced with a long culvert where the river is channelled under the Hwy. 1 Freeway. With a little difficulty, you can put in at Rawlinson road just east of Glover Road and paddle upstream to the Freeway and then down stream to the mouth. Take out at Derby Reach Regional Park about 2.5 km downstream on the Fraser River or paddle up 1.5 km to Fort Langley. A shuttle is required unless you paddle back, which is possible on this slow river. You will also have to portage the dam at the mouth.

This is the river that James McMillan portaged to from the Nicomekl in 1824 to reach the Fraser River and establish an HBC post within the new Canada's boundaries. It was more an attempt to get to the Fraser without having to go around Point Roberts and the treacherous mud flats off the mouth of the Fraser than it was a regular canoe route. There is a cairn noting this in the small park off Glover Road south of the Freeway and another in Portage Park in Langley (see Nicomekl R. on page 54).

The Salmon meets the Fraser about 1.5 km below Fort Langley. An upstream paddle to Fort Langley is on the quieter side channel of the Fraser R. south of McMillan Island. Challenges today that were not there when McMillan did it include the freeway culvert. The other is the dam controlling flood water at the mouth. This river may not be runnable during long dry spells and it may also have vegetation blocking it or at least not presenting a clear channel at any time.

42. SERPENTINE RIVER
•**Location:** Between Mud Bay and Cloverdale.
•**Description:** This is a slow moving tidal river with dikes close
    by obstructing the view from a canoe.
•**Access**: Put in at the King George Hwy. Bridge. No shuttle is
    needed.

You can paddle either way on this slow river. Go the kilometer or two downstream and you pass Ducks Unlimited's Serpentine Fen Bird Sanctuary. Paddle upstream about 14 km (9 mi.) and you see mostly whatever is on the dike banks...grass, cows, blackberries, and wildflowers. The limit for reasonable paddling is Hwy 10. A shuttle trip can launch at Hwy. 10. For a no shuttle trip, always organize so that you are paddling downstream on the way back.

43. SUMAS RIVER
•**Location:** West of Abbotsford.
•**Description:** This is a slow, often meandering river. No
    shuttle needed.
•**Access:** Highway 1 interchange #104 (No. 3 Road). Go west
    1km to Jock MacDonald Park. Launch at the park. Or
    launch at the rest area off Hwy. 1 east of Abbotsford. You
    can paddle in either direction.

Going upstream the river meanders through fields for 6 to 8 km. It may be the runoff from the fields or the local agricultural businesses that contributes to a pretty bad smell there at times. The banks are overgrown with blackberries and in late August, picking from a canoe can reap a bonanza.

Paddling downstream there are fewer meanders as the river follows the largely wilderness foot of Sumas Mountain. Five kilometers downstream is the confluence with the Vedder Canal. Portage over a small dam controlling water levels and continue another 2 km to the Fraser River. Do not paddle into the Fraser as your next take-out is across the river at Dewdney, or just below the Mission Bridge, river left, a distance of 15 km (See Vedder notes for more history)

44. VEDDER RIVER

- **Location:** South of Chilliwack. Take Hwy.1, exit 119 South to Vedder Crossing.
- **Description:** This is a faster flowing stream with some chutes and braiding for about 8 km (5 mi.) It then enters the Vedder Canal for 5 km to the Sumas River. A shuttle is needed.
- **Access:** Put in at the iron bridge at Vedder Crossing. Take out over the dike where the river bends at #3 road (8 km) or at the confluence of the Sumas R. (another 5 km)

The Chilliwack River changes its name at the iron bridge at Vedder Road to become the Vedder River. The entire drainage basin below the bridge borders on a huge swampy shallow lake called Sumas Lake. In the 1920's farmers cooperated to drain the lake and create Sumas Prairie for farmland. The Chilliwack River may have originally wended its way through Chilliwack along Chilliwack River Road. The Vedder may also have been a channel of the Chilliwack as well as drainage for the Sweltzer R. from Cultus Lake. The Vedder Canal is a man-made drainage ditch to handle the flow of these rivers so they do not flood Sumas Prairie. The Chilliwack River Road branch is now just a series of sloughs. Other drainage ditches flow into the Sumas R. which is controlled by a dam.

The Chilliwack R. is for advanced paddlers only. It has flooded regularly in recent years, each time creating different paddling challenges. The Vedder has less drop and is therefore suitable as an easy river. However, there are still chutes, sweepers, gravel bars and some braiding. A dumping is not hazardous in this river. If the water level is low, there may not be enough depth to paddle the Vedder Canal. Do not paddle it in high water.

Intermediate River Day Trips

Most people who have enjoyed the easy river moving-water experience are hooked. You are now entering the more cerebral aspect of the sport. Instead of drifting or paddling lazily, you will now be challenging the river. You will increasingly look for opportunities to do eddy turns, peel offs, and forward and back ferrys. You will become more proficient at spotting shallow gravel bars, finding the best channel as the river braids and knowing how to handle sweepers and strainers.

These intermediate rivers are the next step for you. They are challenging to the point where you will have to use some technical skills to avoid difficulty. But they are also generally forgiving of miscues as there is usually lots of gentle water in which to get rescued. These rivers are generally listed as grade one with some grade two and three rapids. They are all runnable in open canoes, but dumpings do occur so many outfit their boats with flotation of some sort.

Flotation can be as simple as tieing in a

Dogwood Canoe Club members challenge the Similkameen's rapids. Note the air bags and that both paddlers are wearing PFDs and painters are coiled. Dan Wainwright photo.

truck inner tube or blocks of styrofoam, or as elaborate as inflatable air bags made specifically for your type of canoe. PFDs are worn without question and some will have adopted the practice of expert whitewater paddlers of wearing a knife on the PFD for use if they get snagged and have to cut free. Helmets and wetsuits are optional at this level, depending on water temperature and river conditions. Choice of footwear is important. You must wear shoes that will not get ripped off your feet in the current or when swimming and that will let you both swim and walk comfortably on rock and gravel stream beds. High cut runners and wool socks fill the bill. Many wear wetsuit boots that have reinforced soles for walking and zippers for convenience.

At this level, you have to expect to dump at sometime....and it seems it is always when you least expect it. Unless you are wearing a wetsuit, you should carry a change of clothes, matches and "comfort food" in a waterproof container. Cameras must be protected too...some use waterproof padded pouches available commercially, others use ammunition cases or plastic buckets. You will either tie in your gear so it cannot hang down when the canoe is upside down, or you will let it float free and let it be rescued separately. You will also learn to be meticulous in coiling your painters so they are readily available and remain knot free. Many paddlers will carry and learn to use a throw bag. Everyone will know how to do basic canoe-over-canoe rescues and you will learn how to self-rescue in a river.

You should never attempt these rivers without rescue support...three canoes for safety.

45. FRASER RIVER (YALE TO HOPE)

•**Location:** North of Hope B.C.

•**Description:** About 24 km (15 mi.) of grade I river, with many grade II and some grade III rapids.

•**Access:** Put in at either of two river access paths at Yale on Front Street. Turn off Hwy 1 at Albert St. to get to Front. Take out at Hope, river left, just past the Coquihalla R. Line your canoe up the Coquihalla to the Park or get permission to land at Tyelte Yet campsite on Hwy. 1 in Hope.

Do not run this if the river is in flood. All rapids are runnable by intermediate paddlers. 1.5 km below Yale watch for whirlpools. At Emory Creek watch for a grade III chute. Strong headwinds can make this a memorable trip.

46. NORTH ALOUETTE RIVER
•**Location:** North of Haney.
•**Description:** This is a deceptive little river. Tight corners, sweepers, portaging over logs and frequent shallow water. Up to grade II for the first 4.5 km (3 miles), lake grade for the last 4.5 km (3 miles).
•**Access:** Put in at bridge on 224th Street at 132nd Avenue. Park on shoulder. Take out at Harris Road Bridge (192nd Street) Park in large lot at the bridge. Or for a lake grade trip, put in at Harris Road and paddle upstream to where N. Alouette runs too fast, about 1 km east of Neaves Road and then return to put-in.

The upper half of this rain fed stream is best at average water levels as it is too shallow to paddle at low water. If the water level is too high, low branches lacing across the channel may make it a difficult challenging trip. If it is just deep enough at 224th, it is OK. The lower half can be paddled anytime, however it is tidal and is used by power boats in summer. Spring is the best time to go.

The upper half can be challenging but is very interesting as it is treed and wild looking. The lower half is tidal and diked with fields nearby. At this point, the paddler sees little more than the river banks.

Halfway between 208th and 192nd streets, the South Alouette River enters. This river was dammed, creating Alouette Lake and has been reduced to little more than a tidal slough. Paddle up it, but don't waste effort hauling over the logs as it is virtually uncanoeable past that part.

Alouette Lake is a secondary reservoir linked by tunnel to Stave Lake which powers the generators at Stave Falls.

Ice age gravel beds are exposed where there is a current. The lower flood plain has silty shores.The original coastal rainforest of hemlock and cedar has given way to second growth cottonwoods and alder with underbrush of red osier dogwood, willow and salmonberry. Wildflowers such as trillium, ladyslipper orchids and lilies are found in the forested areas in the spring. Beavers live in tunnels in the banks. Waterfowl, songbirds and raptors abound. The silty shores record tracks in good detail. Sandhill cranes are now nesting nearby.

47. SIMILKAMEEN RIVER
- **Location**: Near Princeton B.C.
- **Description:** This is a clean fast river with up to grade II water on many corners and a significant grade III rapid at Golden Dawn. The 40 km (25 mi.) section described is entirely runnable by open canoes in normal water levels.
- **Access:** Put in at the Hwy. 3 bridge east of Princeton. Take out at Stemwinder campsite.

This river is significantly different at high water and must be scouted before attempting as it moves into the Challenging-for-experts category then. Extra flotation is a must. Wetsuits are advisable if the water is cold, but this river warms up nicely in the summer and wetsuits then lead to heat stroke (hyperthermia). July is a good time to play here. It is possible to take out just about anywhere as Hwy. 3 and a forestry access road follow the river on each side.

This four hour drive from the Lower Mainland is too far for a day trip but it lends itself nicely to a weekend of paddling. Run it twice, or play in the best rapids for the whole weekend. There is a free forestry campsite upstream of the Stemwinder bridge on the access road. There are Provincial campsites at Bromley and Stemwinder. The Kelowna Canoe and Kayak Club has erected two biffies on a camping area just below Stemwinder, from which they put on The Pig Race on the first weekend in June....races and a BBQ'd whole pig!

The Similkameen above Princeton has several grade IV and V rapids and is not recommended for open canoes. Below Stemwinder, the river is generally grade II with no significant bigger rapids and is canoeable past the US-Canada border. The take out here is at the river crossing about 20 km south of Keremeos. You can also paddle past Cawston halfway to the border where a bridge gives access to Indian reserve land on the west side. This was an easy take-out at the picnic site, river right, but now you might need a permit from the band. The total canoeable length is about 100 km and would take two to four days depending on how much playing you did in the rapids. Generally, canoes loaded with full camping gear do not play until they unload.

The best plan is to have vehicle support with camping gear meet the playing canoes at day's end.

48. SKAGIT RIVER
  •**Location:** 48 km south of Hope, B.C. on the Silver Creek Road.
  •**Description:** This is a fast river with sweepers and log jams. It
      is only 18 km (10 mi.) long.
  •**Access:** Put in at the bridge across the Skagit River at mile 25
      (km 48). Take out river left before the old logging bridge.
      Best take out is river right at the same place, but the bridge is
      in such disrepair the last time we were there that access to the
      road may not be possible. As usual, scout your access when
      you park your shuttle vehicle.

The Skagit is usually referred to as the BC Skagit to differentiate it from the US Skagit which is also canoeable in Washington, but not from this location. If you canoe past the logging bridge, the river may be impassible due to log debris and low water. Ross Lake is an American reservoir subject to severe draw down. It floods into Canada, but any canoe take-out on Ross Lake will take you across the border where you may have to make special arrangements to get access.

Canoeing this river is a challenge and in highwater can be dangerous. Log jams are frequent and require paddlers to stop and check the route every trip as they frequently change. The river runs fast enough to pin canoes or roll them under the logs. In high water the landing sites are covered and much of the shore is thick underbrush. Dumpings in this river can be serious as clothing can be snagged by branches trapping the swimmer. For this reason, the river has had a sign posting it as unsafe for canoes. However, the canoe clubs paddle it regularly without loss of life and it is considered an intermediate river, but one that requires a prudent cautious approach. It is best paddled when it is closed to fishing to avoid conflict with the anglers.

The Silver Creek Road is not done quickly, which makes it a long drive from the lower mainland. Some do it as a day trip, others prefer a weekend. Camping is unorganized. The put-in has a good camping site for several vehicles or tents.

The B.C. Skagit is a unique micro-climate in that it is similar to our interior drybelt with ponderosa pine and other such drybelt vegetation although it is surrounded by temperate rainforest. It is a flyfisher's paradise as it has some of the best spawning areas for resident trout. For recreation reasons, there was a massive public outcry when Washington applied to raise the level of Ross Dam and flood this canoeable section too. After much publicity, it became politically expedient for the BC government to deny the request.

49. SQUAMISH RIVER (LOWER)
•**Location:** Squamish B.C.
•**Description:** This 40 km (25 mi.) section of the Squamish
    River is generally fast grade I with grade II at some
    corners. It is forgiving of errors, but should not be run while in
    flood.
•**Access:** North of Squamish on Highway 99, take the Cheekye
    exit to go up the Squamish Valley 23 km to the powerhouse.
    Put in there. Take out just past the Mamquam River
    confluence, river left at Squamish.

To find the take out, take the west road to Squamish just south of the Mamquam Bridge. There are one or two unmarked accesses that will let you park close to the dike. Walk over the dike and flag your landing beach. If you overshoot your landing, you will end up in Howe Sound and may experience difficulties paddling to a safe take-out and getting back to your vehicle.

This trip is easily done as a day trip for less experienced intermediate paddlers. There is some maneuvering required at the beginning to stay in the channels and avoid log jams and deadheads. The few standing waves are easily bypassed or run. Much of the trip is just fast grade one water and the scenery is fantastic especially on a fine spring or fall day. Snow-capped peaks, forests, wildlife, fresh air and moderate exercise....no wonder tourists come from all over to see what we've got. The upper section of the Squamish is also canoeable, for experienced paddlers only. See the Challenging Rivers section.

Challenging River Day Trips

The purpose of this book is to provide a variety of paddling experiences for beginning and intermediate open canoe paddlers in B.C.'s Lower Mainland and was compiled to fill a void. There are excellent detailed publications for the whitewater enthusiast, thus the information in this section is largely irrelevant for experienced whitewater paddlers and is only included to show what challenges are available as paddling experience grows.

In this category of paddling, change is constant. These rivers may have substantially altered paddling conditions following any freshet. Channels may straighten, log jams may form, and even though main pools, chutes and ledges do not move, different water levels offer up different conditions to paddlers. The result is a constant challenge.

The equipment for this kind of paddling is specialized. Canoes with substantial rocker allow maximum maneuverability. Solo boats offer better handling in standing waves than do tandem boats. Tandem canoeists will shift the paddlers more to the middle of the canoe to allow more lift in bow and stern. All boats will fill every available space with flotation. The paddlers will wear wet suits and helmets. Even though others are there with throwbag or ready to perform canoe-over-canoe rescues, self-rescues are more the normal pattern when playing in challenging rivers. Self rescues are possible when air bags keep the boat from filling and the paddler can find an eddy or get his feet on the ground.

Open canoes outfitted in this way can challenge the same water that the closed boats tackle. And do!

The inclusion of this category in this book has only three purposes. The first is to warn novice paddlers of the dangers and dissuade them from trying these waters on their own. The second is to show them what kind of adrenaline rush awaits them if they develop their paddling skills. The third is to publicize the fact that we have some world class recreational rivers at our back door and they must not be lost to us for whatever reason.

50. CAPILANO RIVER

•**Location:** North Vancouver

•**Description:** This is Vancouver's very clean drinking water. From the dam to the mouth is only 5.5 km (3.5 mi.) of challenging drops and pools.

•**Access:** Put in near the hatchery at Capilano River Regional Park below Cleveland Dam. Take out at Ambleside Park, river right, at the mouth. For a shorter trip take out river left at Klahanie Park which is below the bridge after the Upper Levels Highway Bridge.

Notes: The water level fluctuates, but there is always some water as they have to maintain a minimum level for the fish. The Capilano was a major spawning stream for salmon. There is a water volume scale painted on the west side of the weir above the hatchery at the put-in. A reading of 3.5 is considered optimum for expert open canoe paddling. Higher water may be run by specialized solo O.C.s with airbags. Lower water exposes concrete and re-bar rubble under the bridges.

This is kayaking water with very tight corners and chutes. The creation of a park meant that the picturesque rugged scenery was maintained. The river can be viewed in many places from the walking trails on the cliffs above and is well worth spending a day just hiking through the woods and watching the kayakers try to avoid wet exits. A trail extends from the hatchery to Ambleside Park. Permits are not yet required, thus anyone can go down the river. Kayakers, canoeists, rafters, tubers and swimmers will all be found here.

An Australian friend of mine had it in his head to go down through Hell's Gate on the Fraser in a dinky raft. I suggested he start on less daunting water and put him and his buddy on the Cap. Their first trip down was exhilarating. "A piece of cake", they said. The second trip down, the Capilano ate the dinky raft and a couple of kayakers hauled them out. I picked up the pieces as they floated by at the mouth. His buddy said he did not believe how green the water looked from the bottom of a pool and his whole life flashed before his eyes before it loosened its grip on him and he bobbed up. They never did get around to rafting Hell's Gate.

51. CHILLIWACK RIVER

•**Location:** South of Chilliwack. Take Hwy. 1 Exit 119 south to Vedder Crossing.

•**Description:** 20 km of world class whitewater.

•**Access:** There are several access points along this very popular river, however those paddling open canoes usually restrict themselves to the lower 7.2 km (4.5 mi.) between Pointa Vista and Vedder Crossing. Put in at the end of Osbourne Road which meets Chilliwack Lake Road at the Pointa Vista Cafe. This has been the traditional put-in but the river has been changing the access and channel location so that adjacent property owners actually own the beach. A more popular put-in is now at Chilliwack River Park which is 6.4 km (4 mi.) upstream of the Vedder Crossing "Iron Bridge". Take out just above the Iron Bridge, river right.

Notes: This river is arguably the best challenging white water in the Lower Mainland. It is also a famous steelheaders' river. There are serious conflicts when fishers and paddlers want to play in the same pool. Common courtesy usually prevails. We don't linger in the pools and the fishers don't cast while we go through.

There are many homes along the river and problems arise with residents when river users create parking congestion, use the bushes as biffies and offend by not stripping off wetsuits discreetly.

Chilliwack River is used by several instructors for their advanced moving water training courses. As well, people come just to raft, tube-float and /or swim it. The Chilliwack is of such importance to organized paddling that it is a designated National Team training location and regularly hosts international paddling competitions.

In the USA, rivers with this appeal and conflict potential are often controlled with a permit system, which effectively eliminates the casual paddler and leaves usage in the hands of the commercial exploiters and organized users. Permits need to be issued and monitored, which means there is a cost which must be borne by the users....and our rivers are no longer free of costs or free to paddle on impulse. It is important that all paddlers understand that it is a privilege, not a right, to paddle our rivers free from bureaucratic entanglements. The fewer the complaints of residents and other users, the farther we will be from legislated control.

My first trip on the Chilliwack was as an eager novice with my son, Dan, paddling bow. It was a DCC family trip and we were the first down to the water at the small beach at Pointa Vista. It was suggested by those experienced club paddlers that we should ferry to the other side and await the others. We did so but as that side got congested, it was suggested that those ready should start. Well, we should never have been lead canoe with the little experience we had, but that is what happened. We had never been down the river before and did not know what to expect, which was probably just as well. Shortly after starting we found ourselves in a series of decent sized standing waves. Dan and I picked and talked our way through them just like we had been taught by Howie Rode. We turned around to see the next two canoes capsized behind us. Then another broached, was momentarily pinned and jackknifed with the bow meeting the stern. A fourth canoe pranged open its bow on a boulder. In all, two canoes were totalled, and two were badly damaged. An Aluminum Grumman capsized a couple of times more on that trip and although it was still afloat, it was not a pretty sight.

This was in pre-canoeing course days and was a powerful incentive for the DCC to support the BCRCA in developing proper courses of instruction. This trip still holds the record for the Dogwood Canoe Club as the most disastrous...and it probably would have been worse if the club had not been so safety conscious. The water was cold and fast, but no injuries occurred, no lives were lost....pride heals and boats can be replaced. And on the plus side, several of those on that fateful trip later served on the BCRCA executive that put such emphasis on paddling courses and safety procedures in BC.

The Chilliwack River changes its name below the iron bridge at Vedder Crossing, to become the Vedder River. It is canoeable to the Fraser, but is not too interesting after it enters the Vedder Canal, so the take-out is usually in Yarrow at Dike Road which is the east end of No. 3 Road.

See the Vedder River on page 59 for more information.

Paddlers in specialized boats regularly challenge the Chilliwack for wildwater experiences from a put-in at Slesse Creek approximately 10 km upstream from the Tamihi Bridge. The Tamihi Bridge is where Chilliwack Lake Road crosses Chilliwack River approximately 10 km upstream from the Iron Bridge at Vedder Crossing.

Any part of the Chilliwack River can change from one freshet to the next. Log jams form and shift. Sweepers come and go. Trees have been known to block the whole river. Twisting runs have straightened out and vice-versa. Paddlers must scout, must not go alone and must proceed with extreme caution following any freshet. There have been no deaths of organized paddlers, but casual users regularly underestimate or are ignorant of the power and dangers of this river which too often is unforgiving.

Challenging the Chilliwack River. Marlin Bayes photo.

52. SQUAMISH RIVER (UPPER)

- **Location:** North of Squamish, B.C.
- **Description:** Fast, cold and unpredictable. Rapids to grade IV. The Squamish is glacier fed so hot weather increases the flow which generally is high June through August, but it also will rise rapidly following heavy rains which may occur any time of year. Open canoes should not run it in high water.
- **Access:** Take Hwy 99 north of Squamish, turn west at the junction to Cheekye (approx. 6 km.); stay left past the bridge over the Chekamus (at Fergies Lodge); continue past the power house (which is the put -in for the lower Squamish run) for 17.5 km to a truck water tower which can be your put-in. Or continue another 14 km to a bridge over the Squamish for your put-in. Take out at any of the downstream put-ins. Flag your take-out so you do not over shoot it.

Notes: The Squamish is a favourite of many paddlers but its flow is unpredictable. Apart from rapids, there is braiding which, if you choose the wrong channel may give you low water difficulties not evident in the adjacent channels. Log jams, sweepers, strainers will all be found along with the Squamish serpents which are long logs which the current keeps submerged for several minutes (or so it seems) and which spring back up suddenly startling the unaware.

It was on this section that we took our new Royalex Mad River Explorer on its maiden trip. We scouted that channel and all agreed our plan of attack seemed the most reasonable route. It was to end with us taking a fast chute between two boulders and swinging into the downstream eddy. All went as planned except no one foresaw that the chute we had lined up so expertly contained a hidden boulder in its grip. We hit that rock so hard that son Dan in the bow almost catapulted out. The surge of water lifted us and our partly swamped canoe clear of the boulder. We did a sluggish eddy turn, landed and inspected the damage. We had a huge bulge in the bow, but because Royalex has a memory, Dan just kicked it out. A round stone punched out the rest of the bulge and that is the way it still is today, 10 years later.

I became a believer in Royalex then. I am positive no other material on the market then could have survived that "brick wall" encounter.

For excellence in scenery, little else will compare to the Squamish. Snow-capped peaks, virgin forests, fast water, interesting paddling challenges....the Squamish has it all.

53. CHEHALIS RIVER
   •**Location:** North of the Harrison River.
   •**Description:** A fast boulder garden challenge made more
      difficult because access to the road is next to impossible once
      on the river.
   •**Access:** take the road to Chehalis Lake off Morris Valley Road
      which is beside Sasquatch Inn .5 km west of the Hwy. 7 bridge
      over the Harrison. The put-in is 16.3 km (10.2 mi.) from the
      Morris Valley junction. It is 1.7 km past the bridge over Statlu
      Creek which is run by closed boaters. Access to the Chehalis
      is via a poor overgrown logging road. It is a 20 minute
      bushwhacking slog. Take-out is at the Morris Valley Road
      Bridge over the Chehalis or paddle on down to the Kilby park
      take-out on the Harrison.
Notes: The canyon part of this run has tempted open boat experts, but not frequently. The put-in is such an ordeal that many are deterred. In fact it was the thought of having to retrace their steps that clouded the judgement of one group who found the water too high for their liking, but started the run anyway. Once started, there is little opportunity to quit but when lives are at stake slogging through thick underbrush is perhaps preferable. The first paddler had difficulty and did not survive.

A second went to assist and was the only one to make it through the whole run. The others, realizing they were powerless to help, fought their way back to the vehicles and went for help at the take out. When you are a participant in high risk activities, there is always the possibility that something will go wrong and deaths will occur. It is probably to the credit of the BC Recreational Canoeing Association's safety and skills programs that such deaths have been minimal in the sport.

Below the bridge take-out on the Morris Valley Road the river is much easier. It braids a bit and has minor log piles, strainers and sweepers. We have used this part of the river as a challenging poling trip. We put in at Kilby Park on the Harrison, paddle up to the mouth of the Chehalis which is 3 km above the Hwy. 7 bridge on river right. (river right is always identified as though you were going downstream.) From there it is 3 km of paddling and poling to reach the Morris Valley Road Bridge. Then you turn around and pole and paddle back to Kilby.

54. SEYMOUR RIVER
•**Location:** North Vancouver.
•**Description:** A challenging river only in high water following heavy rains. Normally it is a 3.7 km grade I and II rock garden from start to finish.
•**Access:** Put in at Swinburne Avenue off Riverside Drive about 1.3 km north of Mount Seymour Parkway for easy access. For a longer run, access is possible another 1/2 km north on Riverside at a public access opposite 2300 Chapman, however, it is 135 stairs to the water and is locked during the summer. Take-out at tidewater past the railway bridge either river right or river left. For the river right take-out, go south at the corner of Mountain Hwy. and Main Street, over the railway tracks, then parallel to the track and under the Second Narrows Bridge to the mouth of the Seymour. For the river left take-out, go south off Main St. on Riverside, then over the railway tracks and west on Spicer parallel to the tracks.

Notes: The Seymour is the best and closest whitewater in Greater Vancouver. As a result it is regularly used for teaching both by our canoe clubs and by Capilano College. The fishers also use it in season as do tubers and summer swimmers so it can at times be a busy overcrowded venue.

There have been regular conflicts between river users and residents. Parking in the residential area put-ins is now severely restricted for non-residents. The locked gate at the Chapman access was a reaction to all night partiers, litter and vandalism. A key is available from Paddle Sports B.C. (formerly Canoe Sport B.C.) but it is only issued to organized groups and requires a hefty deposit.

For a quick evening challenge close to home, the Seymour is fine.

It is a good safe place to sharpen up your moving water skills as there is quick access to help from the many homes along the banks and you can walk out to the road almost anywhere in an emergency.

To avoid a shuttle, it is possible to paddle and line or pole canoes from the take-out well up the river in medium and low water. If the tide is low, the rocks on shore will be covered with greasy-slick algae from just above the railway bridge to the mouth. At low water, an additional hazard is discarded rubble with rebar near the bridges and the remains of old pilings.

In high water the boulders create holes and the riverbank trees become sweepers. The river is now a challenge for expert open canoe paddlers and is no place for novices or intermediate paddlers.

Properly outfitted experts run the Chilliwack River. Marlin Bayes photo.

Wilderness Canoe Camping

Canoe camping as opposed to day tripping means you are travelling by canoe and are self-contained for overnight stays. Whether you go two days or two weeks, you will still have to carry everything you may need for safety and comfort. The only variable will be the amount of food and drink you pack.

Wilderness canoe trippers in British Columbia will experience nature in some of the most exciting settings in the world. The bulk of B.C.'s population is crowded into the Southwest corner of the province. The north is sparsely populated and on many of the trips described in this book, you can go days without seeing signs of other humans. You can be well removed from roads, powerlines, railways and homes. The many mountain ranges in B.C. create scenic vistas. Your pictures will look like calendar art. Wild animals spotted will leave happy memories. You will experience and see the country as it was when the first people arrived. And unfortunately you will see the impact and activities of civilization in areas most people only read about. You will be able to speak about them from first hand observation. You may even become upset and vocal...and you will certainly understand what motivates those that take a stand to preserve the splendor.

Respect is the first rule. Respect the environment, respect the padders in your group and the ones who will follow you. Respect the rights of those that live where you visit. Respect is a theme that should influence how you act on trips and is one that will be found throughout this section on wilderness canoe tripping.

NO TRACE CAMPING ?

On our many trips happy hour has at times found us discussing the pros and cons of no trace camping versus minimal impact camping. The topic is most often triggered when we arrive at a great campsite only to have to clean it up of garbage, poop and toilet paper before we can enjoy it. The experiences and discussions we have had have left a lasting influence on what we do. All our actions aim at no trace camping, but reason and reality dictates minimal impact camping is fine. We arrived at this conclusion when upon leaving a campsite we were all packed and waiting for one individual who was frantically trying to make the grass stand up where her tent had flattened it. What we do has been honed by camping in a variety of conditions and modified as needed. What follows is what we do in normal wilderness circumstances.

GARBAGE DISPOSAL

One of our lengthy discussions set the direction for our handling of garbage. We really came to a firm decision after having to dig two deep pits on the Athabasca River to bury the garbage of previous campers. We had been packing out what we had packed in, but while that was fine for what we carried, we could not do that for what we found on site. We rationalized that everything we packed out would just go into a sanitary land fill somewhere. We further rationalized that if we did it right, we could handle it on site better than a landfill could.

A quiet moment in camp. Marlin Bayes photo.

We knew that bacterial action only works in the upper layers of soil in the presence of air. We knew that air oxidizes metals. We knew that animals would dig up and scatter any garbage with any vestige of food remaining. We knew that glass and plastic would not break down. So, what we do as routine is burn in our evening campfire all cans, papers and food scraps including orange peels and apple cores. We try not to carry glass containers and we pack out all clean plastic and burn the impossible-to-clean plastics. We know the burning of plastic is harmful to the atmosphere but food scraps also entice and encourage forays by wildlife that may be more harmful in other ways.

In the morning we scrape the remains of our cans out of the ashes, flatten them and deposit them in the biffy hole. We then refill the hole and return the plug of vegetation to make it as natural as possible. In locations where the cans may be uncovered by flooding, we pack them out. After all, no one wants to roam a beach looking for pretty rocks and find crushed cans...it takes the romance out of the moment.

If in doubt, pack it out.

CAMPFIRES

Everyone knows to build their cooking fire on ground that will not burn. Over the years we have come across many fires that were still smoldering in roots. We have had to clean tent sites of charcoal and ashes before we could use them. We landed at one site on the Peace River that had been a campsite for friends of ours five years earlier. We easily recreated their camp from the fire rings of rocks that had been left behind. All these experiences have again influenced what we do.

We make one communal campfire location at each camp. It is often located some distance from the tents as our kitchens need not be near the sleeping areas. Food is never kept anywhere near the tents. We make sure there will be adequate space for all our lawn chairs around the fire, remove and save the vegetative layer of soil and dig down to the mineral layer. We do not use rocks for fire rings as we have found that steel grates with folding legs do a better job. They let us keep the fire small and feed it from all sides.

Our cooking fire is small. One grate will handle the pots for three pairs of campers, two grates is the most ever needed. After everyone has done their cooking, we remove the grates, build up the fire, burn our garbage and carry on with Happy Hour campfire activities.

On departure, we make sure the fire is out with generous dousing from our bailers and then return it to as natural a state as possible by replacing the vegetative layer we removed. More often our fire is built out on sand and gravel bars where the next high water will rearrange and reclaim it anyway. We don't use logs to create a fire pit.

The old outdoors manuals of the early 1900s were badly out of step with today's reality. They exploited the land and too often left a lasting impression. Scouting has long since embraced a policy of no-trace camping. Other organized groups have also done an admirable job of educating members. However, we still come across this old time mentality. Campers have slashed evergreens to make soft beds then left them in place. Tent and tarp poles have been lashed and left for *the next user*. In reality, the *next user* does not want to be reminded of those that have gone before. We now carry Thermarest mattresses which are much better than any bed of boughs. We use ropes to support tarps and carry telescoping poles to prop up the corners. We never drive nails into the trees to hang stuff on. We will scrounge, cut and lash deadwood branches to make a kitchen counter workplace at convenient height but it is all returned to nature before we leave. Unused firewood is scattered too. Part of the fun in camping is to create a comfortable nest out of stuff scrounged but you almost feel like an intruder if it is all stacked there for you.

Canoe camping in comfort. Marlin Bayes photo.

SURVIVAL KITS

Much has been written on how to survive in the bush and what should go into a survival kit. If you ever get into that situation when canoeing, it will be because you have capsized and have lost everything not attached to you.

With that in mind the wilderness paddler should carry specific items with him at all times. Our minimum list includes:

- A belt knife
- A large, red handerkerchief
- A belt pouch holding
  - flint & steel and tinder (Coghlans)
  - good compass
  - personal medications and a few ASA
  - a few bandaids

Our reasoning for a minimal kit is that it will be carried whereas a bulky one will end up in a pack. Our choice of items reflects the reality that a surviving wilderness paddler's greatest need is to get dry and warm and tend to any injuries. It will not be long before searchers start to look for you but it may take several days before you're found. You can go days without food and even a few days without water. Getting water should not be a big problem; purifying it might be.

The belt knife can be used for making kindling and carving bark to fashion a cup.

The large handerchief can act as a bandage, head covering, or even water strainer. Strips from a red one can flag a trail for searchers.

Coghlan's fire tinder kit lights readily even when wet. A fire, of course, dries the paddler, dispels the night somewhat, acts as a beacon for searchers and is psychologically satisfying. If you know how Indians heated rocks so they could cook food in wooden boxes, you might even be able to make hot tea flavoured with evergreen tips after you make a bark cup.

The compass will only be needed if you have to hike out and are reasonably sure where to go.

Personal medications and ASA help you maintain health and so minimize panic decisions. Bandaids help keep minor cuts clean.

BEAR FACTS AND OTHER WILDLIFE

Respect (there is no other word for it) is immediately impressed on campers encountering a bear. Other animals invoke curiosity and a dash for the camera. Bear encounters just trigger the dash. Why?

Canoe campers in B.C. will often see a bear on a wilderness trip. Trippers in a Provincial Park where all wildlife is protected may have the unfortunate experience of meeting a camp bear. These beasts have absolutely no fear of anything. Whistles, clanging pots, a kick on the rump are all shrugged off as he helps himself to your food pack, or anything that smells like food. The park campsites all have high platforms where you can stash your food, with removable ladders to reach them. But these smart animals do not necessarily leave you the opportunity. In fact they have been known to meet you on the beach and help you unload! There is little you can do to protect yourself from these marauders apart from being vigilant, always separating all food from non-food gear and getting your food buckets out of their reach as soon as possible. Make sure you don't leave the ladder up either. Most camp bears roam the area at night, but many have found it more profitable to adjust their meal hours to coincide with yours.

Wary wolverine heads for home. Marlin Bayes photo.

As a matter of practice, we religiously separate foods from other gear. This gives us discrete packages to hoist and keeps all smell of food away from our sleeping gear. We most often set up our kitchen area away from our sleeping area so if we do have a nocturnal visitor, it is less likely to bother our tents. All our foods are stored in their own waterproof containers, either repacked in reusable plastic jars or in their original foil or plastic wrap. These containers are then stored in wooden boxes with tight lids or plastic buckets with tight lids. The only time I used a soft pack for food, mice vandalized it. Even if you never have a bear encounter, you'll never have a trip where mice or other gnawers won't explore your camp as you sleep.

On our many trips detailed in this book, bears have never been a problem. Outside the protected park boundaries, any bear that chanced on our camp hightailed it as soon as it scented humans. These bears have never had the luxury of being protected and many have had unpleasant or deadly encounters with hunters. A lot of folks in the North find bear tasty.

To hoist up your food where there is no platform, sling a rope between two trees as described in the way to set up a biffy tarp on page 83. Use a carabiner as a pulley or tie the food containers on and hoist them up. This is easier said than done as ropes sag and food packages are heavy. Bears can climb trees easily and can reach up over 3 m from the ground so be especially conscientious in your food caching.

FIREARMS FOR PROTECTION?

We have found that the presence of people keeps most bears away. On a trip on the upper Fraser, we saw 16 bears in 14 days. Only one lingered long enough to get his picture taken and that was only because we saw him before he sensed us. On the North Thompson and on the Fort Nelson we have startled bears who actually galloped off throwing up sprays of gravel.

The only time we took a firearm for protection was on the lower Stikine River. I phoned Alaska Fish and Game Dept., told them we were planning to do the Stikine in August and asked their advice. The fellow fairly shouted that he would not do it without a very big gun.

I asked what permits were needed. He said none unless I shot something. He indicated that the ensuing paperwork was horrendous.

So I took my 30.06 in its hard cover case. The only time I took it out was to show customs in Prince Rupert. We saw several bears on the trip and stopped at one location where we found a huge fresh grizzly bear track measuring over 14 inches long! Some of us then bushwacked our way in to a lake while the others had a long lunchbreak on the other side. When we met up, a black bear ambled out of the bush behind them. He had probably been there all along. And the other half of the group said they watched us disappear into the bush while a huge grizzly appeared behind us just fifty feet upstream. Aside from the track, we did not know he was there but with all the noise we deliberately made, there was no misunderstanding that he knew exactly where we were. And my rifle? Well it was safely stowed in its case in the bottom of my canoe.

More often than not we see only the evidence of big animals because we usually don't get on the river until 9:30 a.m. or so. On all our northern B.C. trips we saw moose tracks, huge wolf tracks, bear, fox, skunk and beaver tracks. Rarely did we ever see the animal actually making them. We even saw a badger on the Thompson River once. A good reference book on animal tracks will add to your trip's enjoyment. On the Fort Nelson/Liard river trip we saw what we thought were caribou tracks only to find out later that a herd of wood bison had naturalized in the area. Wood bison have tracks similar to caribou so we were never really sure of exactly what we saw.

In summary, wild animals are not a threat to the wilderness canoe camper in B.C. as long as reasonable precautions are taken.

BEAR SPRAY

If you are still concerned about bears, take along bear spray (Capsicum pepper derivative) which is legal in Canada for use on dangerous animals. It is sold in outdoor shops and is a 10 percent pepper solution that will incapacitate a bear. It will also incapacitate the user if the wind drifts it back. Although the effects wear off in about 45 minutes, contact lens wearers may suffer serious problems.

BIFFIES

Respect for privacy and a desire to maintain a clean camp dictates our next topic. In a group of three to six canoes, you have six to twelve people who will have to find a place where they can meet nature's call.

When you realize that other paddlers will find that campsite just as you did, you will see that there is a lot of people-pressure on a few key sites in the wilderness. When we scouted out the Stuart and Nechako rivers for a Parks Canada Fur Brigade reenactment, our greatest concern after finding sites for fifty tents each night was establishing proper biffies.

In the Dogwood Canoe Club, we even sing about it. The chorus of our annual activities summary song is: "In a jiffy we'll build you a biffy to sit in and sing along, too."

Now here, for the first time in print is our Spiffy Jiffy Biffy. We use the light nylon fly from an old tent. Its size of 10'x12' is versatile for various situations. A hundred feet of rope with a weight, a few tent pegs and a 36" hoop of stiff wire complete the outfit. All but the hoop stuffs compactly into a light daypack and stows easily in the canoe.

To set up the biffy, select two trees with branches ten or twelve feet up and a big enough space between them for the biffy. Throw each end of the rope over the branches using a weight to carry it through the air eliminating the need for climbing. Tossing the rope up through the branches is easily done with a weight on each end. And, because the rope is long, it can be tied off at ground level or wherever convenient. The sag in the rope lets you tie on the tarp from the ground, then it is simply hoisted to the desired height. Taking it down is even easier. Untie each end of the rope and it comes down by itself.

Use the same system to put up a rope to hoist up your food. A carabiner on the rope will act as a pulley and make it easier to hoist heavy food buckets.

Dig a small 18" deep hole under the line of the rope where there will be fewer roots, making sure to save the plug of vegetation removed for no-trace replacement after.

The biffy tarp may be erected several ways. If rain shelter is needed, set it up like a tent with the hoop giving it shape about six feet above the ground and the opening away from the camp. Use tent pegs or shovels of dirt to anchor the base. Our old tent fly has a couple of loops conveniently placed to tie the hoop in.

The biffy tarp may also be erected as a lean-to or as a sheet wall depending on the available trees and the weather expected. We have even erected it on sand bars by anchoring three paddles with the rope and pegs and used them to support the tarp to give two walls for privacy.

The U.S. National Parks have a policy of no trace camping, consequently biffies cannot be dug. River users must use a bucket or ammo case that is lined with plastic bags. All feces and toilet paper must be packed out and rangers check at the take-out to make sure you comply. They will let you urinate in the river or on wet sand so the packed-out load is lighter.

Our national parks do not have the same requirement. On the Broken Islands section of Pacific Rim National Park, you must camp in designated sites where they have provided biffies. They have recently been installing solar powered composting outhouses that cost $19,000 each.

B.C. Parks and B.C. Forest Service both provide outhouses at their advertised campsites.

Maps, Charts and Tables

DAY TRIP MAPS

For casual day trips, a good road map is sufficient to find your access points. The map we have included is approximately 2.5 km per centimeter. The access points are indicated by arrows. This book has omitted the obvious routes to the put-ins and take-outs as the map is a much more graphic indicator. Where an access may be obscure, we have added more detail in the text.

WILDERNESS CANOE CAMPING MAPS

Accurate maps are essential on wilderness trips. We cannot do better than the Canadian Government's official topographic maps. These come in two scales. The 1:50,000 is about 4/5 of a mile per inch or .5 km per cm . It gives great detail, but you need a great many pages to cover a 7 to 10 day trip which makes for a bulky and expensive package.

The official topographic maps with a scale of 1: 250,000 are approximately 4 miles to the inch or 2.5 km per cm . They give the same basic information as the larger scale map. They note rapids, waterfalls, weirs, dams, and braiding. No map can be totally accurate as to river position as they are not updated after each flood. Moving hazards such as log piles and gravel bars cannot be charted. Buildings are indicated, but there is no guarantee they will still be occupied or standing. The elevation contour lines give a general indication of possible canyons and possible campsites or landing areas. The maps also show creeks which might be good for drinking water. Topo maps help you gauge your trip so you get off the river when you said you would, thus avoiding the embarassment and expense of a search party. For canoe camping the 1:250,000 scale is adequate.

In the text on each trip we note the 1:250,000 maps and charts you will need to order from: **Map Distribution Office, Department of Energy, Mines and Resources, 615 Booth Street, Ottawa, Ontario**

These maps are also available from government publication stores in the larger Canadian centers.

TIDEWATER TRIPS

Tidewater trips require more information than do river trips. The ocean is generally lake grade until you start paddling in channels. At this point, tidewater acts much like a river. You may paddle along with a 7 knot current and then not be able to paddle back. Then the tide changes and the current reverses its flow. Severe tide rips are no place for a loaded camping canoe. On all tidewater trips you must have reasonably accurate Tide Tables and Current Charts. You also need the Navigation Charts for your trip area. Navigation charts indicate current strength and direction. They show the shoreline to help you find campsites. And they show drying mud flats that you want to avoid. Navigation charts also show the location of lights and channel markers as well as important landmarks. A slow moving craft such as a canoe can be thrown well off course by unseen currents, especially when vision is obscured by rain, mist or fog. A compass and the knowledge to use it along with the charts may be the difference in keeping on course.

Navigation Charts and Tide and Current Tables are all available from any store specializing in outfitting yachters and are readily found in the Yellow Pages or from the Map Distribution Office above. Tide and Current Tables Volume 5 covers Juan de Fuca and Straits of Georgia. Volume 6 covers the rest of the B.C. Coast.

Topographic maps stop at tidewater and so do not give the detail of Navigation Charts, but they do help you name the mountains you see, plan on-shore hikes and generally help in satisfying your curiosity of your surroundings.

It is not the purpose of this book to teach you to read a compass, chart, map or table. We urge that you acquire these skills on your own.

I have my own definition of LOST which you are welcome to use. Lost is when someone has to come and find you. Bewildered is when you are not sure where you are, but you figure it out on your own. I admit to being bewildered many times, almost to the point of not making it back by nightfall, but I adamantly deny that I've ever been LOST.

OTHER HELPFUL MAPS

The **Outdoor Recreation Council** has published an excellent series of maps covering several recreation areas in B.C. They indicate recreation trails and campsites often not noted elsewhere. Order their catalogue of publications from: **Sport B.C. Building, 1367 West Broadway, Vancouver, B.C.**

They are also available from any large store catering to outdoor recreation.

The **B.C. Forest Service** also produces a series of free maps covering all of B.C. in enough detail to find your way down logging and forest access roads to their free Forestry Campsites. The Forestry campsites are invariably on accessible lakes and rivers. They provide a biffy, garbage can and tent or vehicle campsites. Get these maps at official Tourist Information Centers, Local Forestry offices, Government Agents or order them from The Forestry Service in Victoria. They will not send you a full set of maps, so be specific as to the area you want.

The map we have included is in enough detail to indicate the put-ins and take-outs for our Lower Mainland day trips. While it is adequate for day trips, it is not accurate enough to locate specific camping areas and topographical features. Only roads important for accessing paddling waters are shown.

COMPASS AND RULER

Carry a good compact liquid damped magnetic compass with transparent base and rotating bezel. If your compass does not have a straight edge with cm or inches on it, carry a small ruler. The ruled scale helps you measure distances accurately. The straight edge helps you line up landmarks or navigation points.

Lazy day paddling. Dan Wainwright photo.

Canoe Camping Travel Needs

Canoe Camping is a cross between backpacking and tailgate camping. You can carry many more creature comforts than you can going "backpacking light". On the other hand, there are limitations. The checklist included on page 100 is not meant to be a prescription, but rather a suggestion of items to be considered. Most items will be on most trips and you may also have a few more things important to you that are not on the list. Customize the list with your own additions in the blank spaces provided. It may not be readily apparent why an item is included, so the following chapter is an explanation, and includes packing tips where that is important.

CANOE: Maintain a minimum of 7 inches freeboard when fully loaded with people and gear. A 16 foot canoe with broad beam is considered minimal and most canoe campers prefer more length for the extra speed and ease of paddling and packing. Canoe design should also be appropriate for the waters to be paddled.

Most of my trips have been in a 17.5' Clipper Tripper ultralight. It is fast, roomy and fine for water to grade II. My first trip was in a 15 foot Greenwood wood and canvas canoe, which was wanting for freeboard and space. Our 18 foot Greenwood which replaced it is great for ocean trips, but it weighs over 90 lbs. and is impossible to maneuver in rivers. Our last trip was in a Clipper Prospector 17 foot ultralight, chosen for its ability to maneuver in the river, pack a load and ride up on the waves. It is slightly slower than the Tripper, but safer in big water.

PADDLES: One per paddler and one spare. Make sure they are the right length for you. Too short or too long and you will be doing far more work than needed. You should feel comfortable with one hand on the grip and the other holding the shaft close to the blade while you are paddling. A lighter paddle eases the effort and wood or plastic is fine as long as it is stiff enough to resist bending as you paddle.

PAINTERS: 8 mm (3/8") floating ropes tied on bow and stern (braided polyproplene is best). Recommended length is anywhere between the length of the canoe to 8 m (25 ft.). Install grab loops on bow and stern to facilitate attaching painters when you are using a spray cover.

BAILER: Use a scoop made by cutting down an empty plastic bleach bottle with the lid on. Other uses include using it for dousing campfires.

SPONGE: A large sponge is useful to get the water that the bailer misses. It is also great for wiping forest debris off the bottom of your tent or ground sheet when packing up.

SPRAYCOVER: This is used more to reduce wind drag, improve appearances and turn away minor waves and rain than it is to create a covered boat capable of crashing through heavy water. In lieu of a spraycover, use a plastic tarp tucked in tightly around your load.

LOCK, KEY, CABLE: Whenever you leave your boat unattended whether it is on your car or on a beach, it is a good idea to lock it. A locked canoe cannot drift off on an incoming tide, sail away on a strong wind or be pilfered by opportunists. Use a bicycle cable, padlock...and don't forget or lose the key. Two or three canoes can be tethered together with one cable.

THROW BAG and CARABINERS: Used for rescue in river dumpings, freeing pinned canoes...can also be used to cache food away from bears.

PFDs: Personal Flotation Devices must fit like clothing and be comfortable enough to wear while sitting paddling. They are often worn on shore for warmth, especially under a nylon shell or rain parka.

WHISTLE: Get a good loud one that works when wet. Attach it to your PFD zipper. Take it on your hikes in the bush, too in case you go astray.

MAPS OR CHARTS: Always get the official government maps for your trip area. 1:250,000 (2.5 kms per cm) is barely adequate. These maps note major rapids, canyons and mud flats. They help you locate drinking water. They note dwellings where there may be people. And they help you pace your trip so you get back at the time you told people you would return.

COMPASS: This is essential if you are on ocean or big lake waters where you may have fog and currents....or if you are hiking away from the river.

TENT: You can go with a sheet of plastic but what are you trying to prove? Take your tent, either high-tech dome or an old nylon house tent like mine, to shelter you. Don't forget the poles and ropes and have an emergency plan should a pole or grommet break or be lost. Don't forget the tent fly which can make a big difference in keeping you dry in rain and cool in heat.

KITCHEN TARP: A 12'x12' reinforced plastic tarp makes a good shelter for an outdoor cooking, eating and socializing area. Spare tent poles make erection easy and 1/4" rope is strong yet compact enough so a lot takes up little space.

BIFFY TARP: Three canoes for safety, means six people will have to find convenience and privacy to defecate in camp. A camp biffy solves the problem. Use a light nylon fly, a hoop for shape and a 30 m rope as shown on page 83. Take a decent shovel too.

TOOLS: You only need one shovel, axe and saw per group.

AXE: Use for cutting firewood, pounding tent pegs, flattening cans...make sure it starts sharp. A 3/4 size axe is usually sufficient.

SHOVEL: Use for digging the biffy hole, leveling tent sites, covering campfire.

SAW: Use for cutting firewood.

VISE GRIPS: Handy for clamping items needing repair, acts as a pot handle, fish hook remover.

DUCT TAPE: Use to repair canoes, paddles, tents.

STRING: handy for lashings, clothes line.

WORK GLOVES: Use to avoid burns at the campfire, splinters and blisters, all of which can make paddling painful.

SWISS ARMY KNIFE: A good one (not a cheap imitation) can have features that will replace other implements. Use it as a screwdriver, can opener, awl.

FLASHLIGHT: You won't believe how dark the nights can be! Take spare batteries & bulb.

CANDLE: Saves the flashlight. Acts as fire starter, too. Take a thick parafin one.

NEEDLE AND THREAD: Use for clothing and gear repair. Take a needle with an eye big enough for dental floss as that makes a strong thread.

FIRST AID KIT: Know how to properly use the items you take.

BANDAIDS: Take an assortment of sizes and a few butterfly ones.

GAUZE PADS: 2" or 3" is adequate. A sanitary napkin works well in an emergency.

ADHESIVE TAPE: One inch wide is versatile. Wrap it on a pill bottle if you have to conserve space.

BANDAGE: A roll of 2" gauze bandage will handle most wounds.

TENSOR BANDAGE: Helps ease strained joints.

COTTON BATTING: To swab wounds and apply disinfectant.

DISINFECTANT: Zephrin is non-sting. Water based Iodine can also be used as a water purifier. Polysporin disinfects and speeds healing.

BAKING SODA: Relieves insect stings, heartburn.

SCISSORS: To cut gauze, trim nails.

TWEEZERS: Use to remove splinters.

PERSONAL items are just that. Carry your own in your clothing bucket.

TOILET PAPER: Moss is messy, scratchy and damages the environment!

MEDICATIONS: Prescriptions and over-the-counter medications. For essentials like insulin, have extra supplies carried in a different canoe.

ASPIRIN: Or your usual headache remedy.

ANTACIDS: To counter mild heartburn.

SOAP, WASHCLOTH, TOWEL: For washing up.

DEODORANT: To remain on friendly terms with the others.

HAIR FIXIN'S: Whatever it takes.

RAZOR: For a clean shave?

TOOTH BRUSH, PASTE, DENTAL FLOSS: unless you soak 'em at night.

HAND LOTION, LIP CHAP STICK: ...never know when you'll meet Mr. Right, right?

MIRROR: Refuse to look in it on a camping trip? Well then take it just for use as an emergency signal.

WRIST WATCH: If you know the time and can see the sun, you can tell directions.

READING GLASSES, SUN GLASSES: Have spares, too.

SUN SCREEN, SUN BLOCK: Sunny days on the river can burn you up.

INSECT REPELLENT: Camp on gravel bars and drier sites to minimize the flying biters.

SLEEPING: Get a good night's sleep and keep your cheery disposition. All the sleeping gear for the two of us we store in one large waterproof bag with carrying straps.

SLEEPING BAG: Make sure it is rated for the conditions you expect, otherwise you'll be sleeping fully dressed...which makes you feel clammy all day. The new synthetics dry quickly, feather down doesn't.

THERMAREST mattresses self inflate, level uneven ground and are very comfortable. You can swim with them, too.

PILLOW: Take a pillow case and stuff a jacket or other clothing inside to make a pillow.

SLEEPWEAR: Consider that nature will call you at night, or as happened to us on the Athabaska River, a Helicopter dropped two geologists off on the next bar at daybreak. Talk about emptying tents in a hurry....very interesting what people wear or don't wear at night.

CLOTHING The campers rule is be prepared, keep dry and dress in layers. Each paddler is limited to one five gallon bucket for clothing and personal gear. Rain gear is stored separately so as to be easily at hand.

WATER WEAR: On-water wear must not chafe or bind. Pay particular attention to bras and PFDs. For footwear try to get high top waterproof boots. Yachter's boots work well and are light enough to swim in. Wet suit boots are often used on day trips, but on canoe camping trips, your feet will stay wet all day for days at a time, which leads to medical problems. An alternative is to wear high top runners and put clean dry wool socks on every day. The shoes will be damp, but the dry socks will minimize the discomfort and wool retains good insulating value when wet. Paddlers do not play in the river with fully loaded canoes so dumping is a rarity, but walking in shallows is a daily occurance. Thus if compromises must be made, go with having dry feet in shallow water and give up ease of swimming with boots on.

ON-LAND WEAR: It is a comfort to change into light, dry sneakers once camped, but rain and heavy dew may preclude that. You may have to don dry socks and your "on-water" boots. Otherwise dress for the weather.

WARM DAYS: Wear a light shirt. Long sleeves help ward off sun and mosquitoes. Light weight pants help in the cover up. Shorts can double as swimwear. A cap with a visor is a must for most of us. Light socks and sneakers give on-land comfort.

COOL WINDS: Add a wool sweater and a light nylon shell with a hood type collar. These layers will minimize the wind chill, let you protect the back of your neck and add insulation. A nylon shell will also turn away light rain and dry quickly. Consider getting one large enough to wear over your PFD. Avoid heavy insulated waterproof jackets because you cannot adjust the insulating factor and your paddling effort will leave your inner layers wet and clammy. Polypropylene underwear wicks moisture away from your body, keeping you drier. You do not normally need it when paddling, but you might consider it if strenuous hiking is on your agenda.

COLD EVENINGS: Wear wool, if possible. A heavy shirt, sweater and poly-fleece jacket may all be needed. Pants of heavier weight cotton drill or stretch jeans withstand snags and sparks yet dry quickly. Blue jean denim takes forever to dry. Panty hose, polypropylene long johns or fleece sweat pants can be worn as underwear for added layers of insulation. A toque will keep the head warm. All of these including your PFD can be worn as layers if the weather turns cold on you. Keep in mind that the synthetic fleeces do not absorb water and so give good insulation after they are wrung or shaken out. However, they get neat holes from campfire sparks, and may burn well too. Wool withstands sparks and flames better and although damp when wrung out, still retains some insulation value. Gloves or mitts are not generally worn while paddling as they are more of a liability when wet, but you might wish to consider them for cold evenings on land. Most of us, however, just warm our hands in our pockets or armpits when they are not wrapped around a hot drink. Dry wool socks can also double as mitts in an emergency.

RAIN RAIN RAIN: Be a pessimist when packing and consider that you may be a hundred miles from shelter and out in heavy, continuous rain. Waterproof, breathable outer wear is a must. Clean GORE•TEX®-type materials work well. Their semi-permeable fabrics allow water vapour to escape but block the passage of larger water molecules from wetting you. However, their effectiveness is destroyed by dirt or oils. Coated synthetics keep the water out, but do not breathe so the best have ventilation built in across the back, chest, armpits and crotch. A hood worn over a baseball cap or toque keeps the head and neck dry. Suspenders will keep the pants up. An all purpose canvas hat with brim will keep your head dry and warm and will also ward off sun and heat should you be so lucky as to suffer that kind of weather.

OTHER CLOTHING: A few items of clothing don't fit the other catagories too well. Take a couple of large handkerchiefs. They can be used as sweatbands, head scarfs, pot holders, bikinis, bandages and nose wipers. If mosquitoes like you, take a mosquito netting hat and lots of repellent. For sleepwear, consider pyjamas that can double as longjohns underwear. Take swimwear as you can't always indulge in bare bottom nudity. And if hiking is a possibility, pack proper hiking footwear.

RECREATIONAL EQUIPMENT: This is what it is all about, right?

Let's start with happy hour and rest and relaxation. Most of us no longer care if we exude a macho image. We are more concerned with easing an aching back that is doing unaccustomed tasks. The answer we have found is to pack a comfortable folding **LAWNCHAIR**. Choose one that folds fairly flat, that has woven plastic bands that wipe dry, that has good back support, is light and will stow in your canoe. The common folding chair will usually suffice. Avoid taking an old one that is going to collapse the second time you sit in it on uneven ground. Any canoe that is large enough for canoe camping will easily stow a couple of camp chairs and still leave the canoe with a low profile.

You can't be on water all day and not try catching a few fish for supper. Take a telescoping backpack type **ROD**, spinning **REEL** and an assortment of **TACKLE** likely to entice the fish in that area. Do not forget to check the regulations and get the proper **PERMITS** either. You never know when a Conservation Officer will appear. We were on the rugged coast off the Queen Charlottes when a Coast Guard ship appeared and a zodiac intercepted us. All our "papers" were in order. We even had written permission from the Haidas to visit their abandoned village sites.

You also may want **BINOCULARS** and **REFERENCE BOOKS** to identify the strange new flora and fauna. And of course you'll have to record the trip so you can impress (bore?) your sedentary friends with your adventures so take a **CAMERA** and plenty of **FILM**; a **JOURNAL** with **PEN** and **PENCILS**; and even a **SKETCHBOOK** if you are so adept.

Do not forget a **DAYPACK** to take all the stuff you need on hikes.

A deck of **CARDS**, a **NOVEL**, **CROSSWORDS**, **GAMES**, help fill rainy days and quiet times. **MUSICAL INSTRUMENTS** add to campfire sing-a-longs.

The CANOE CAMPING KITCHEN:

Just because you are on vacation doesn't mean you can ignore the chores of meal making and cleanup but the right tools and a little organization can make it a lot easier. Everything listed below except the grate I pack in one 5 gallon bucket labelled *"KITCHEN"*. The bucket lid is our cutting board.

On the bottom is a single burner **STOVE** and cylinder of **FUEL**. I prefer to cook over an open fire on these trips, but every so often we encounter a ban on fires or wet miserable weather when we'd rather cook under cover. For the open fire a good grate is convenient. You can use an old oven rack or buy a **HEAVY DUTY WIRE GRATE** with legs so you don't have to balance it on rocks.

On top of the stove sits a **NEST OF POTS**; one is a billy can for coffee; one large pot boils water for washing and heating "magic pantry" packages; another is used for pastas and veggies while the last one is kept clean of soot for use as a mixing bowl.

Two **BOWLS** and two **MUGS** nest in the billy can. The lids act as serving dishes or trays, but are too thin to be used as frying pans.

Instead, we found a **FRYING PAN** with a handle that unscrews so it can sit on the pots in our kitchen bucket. The two dinner **PLATES**, the cloth bag holding **CUTLERY, LIFTER, WOODEN SPOON, CAN OPENER, MATCHES, LIGHTER, HANDLES** and the **DISH TOWEL** and **CLOTH** in its plastic bag all fit into the frying pan. The **SOAP, SCRUBBER,** and **FILLETING KNIFE** slip down the sides and a pair of work gloves for use around the fire tops off the package.

Our second kitchen container is a thin walled **BOX** about 18"x12"x10"h. It has a removable plywood lid held in place with suitcase snaps. The lid acts as a flat work surface and the box makes everything conveniently at hand. The contents are all in their own waterproof **PLASTIC CONTAINERS**. The box holds all the condiments, staples, beverage powders, some of the food and things like foil, extra ziploc bags and paper towels. Carry a few **GARBAGE BAGS** because they can double as rain coats and ground sheets. See the checklist for other kitchen needs.

A smaller **BUCKET** holds our lunch for the day plus other things we may want at hand, such as sunscreen, sunglasses, binoculars, first aid kit, beverages and sharing foods such as gorp or hard candy. Other buckets and the **DAY PACK** hold the rest of the food.

WATER is an essential to carry on most trips. We use two 10 l (2.5 gal) collapsible plastic containers. When one is empty, we refill it at a stream enroute and treat it with Iodine or Chlorine bleach. They stow easily in the canoe. See appendix for water treatment details.

MEAL PLANNING

Keeping in mind that this is a holiday trip, we have looked for foods convenient to cook and store. The Magic Pantry dinners have solved most of that problem. But on layover days it is nice to have a change by cooking a pasta, veggies and anything else you choose. Some in our group plan out each meal in advance. We do not. Instead, we take food for 12 days if that is the length of the trip and then decide what we feel like eating. We usually have food left over because we eat fish on one or two occasions.

The foods as we have listed them on the checklist are according to the meal when we usually eat them. A few explanations are needed.

MAGIC PANTRY® or similar foil packed meals do not need

refrigeration and can be heated in their pouch in a pot of boiling water. The pouch can even serve as the bowl and the boiled water used to make tea. The microwave versions are bulkier, but they still heat up well in boiling water and the tray can be used as a bowl.

FRESH FOODS that store and travel well are oranges, carrots, onions and potatoes. But, they are bulkier than their instant alternatives, so limit them to days when you have lots of time to cook or eat them raw. A few prunes daily make up for the change in diet and maintain regularity. On our last trip, raw turnip was a hit as a Happy Hour finger food.

Meals for the first day or two can be perishable foods that you can not keep. One trick is to start with frozen meat which will be thawed for day two.

The best **BREAD** we have found is Venice Bakeries' Oberlander Rye. One unsliced loaf of this does the two of us for a week's lunches of cheese sandwiches. So-called soft margarine will turn to oil on warm days so stay with the harder stuff.

BISCUIT MIX can be used for making pancakes or biscuits in the frying pan, or dumplings in soup or stew. Add freshly picked berries for a treat.

Happy hour beverages include **BEER in CANS**, overproof **RUM** in a plastic bottle, **TEA and COFFEE**. Try hot chocolate and triple sec! Sharing snacks include **PEANUTS** in the shell because they go a long way.

Foods packed at the bottom of the canoe remain cool. **A WET SACK** will keep things cooler through evaporation. Beverage cans can be put in a stream in a **MESH BAG** or landing net to keep them from floating off while they cool.

Ice cream is out, but we have found we can make **INSTANT PUDDINGS** and even cheesecake on layover days.

Canoe Camping Checklist

TRAVEL
- ❑ canoe
- ❑ paddles
- ❑ painters
- ❑ bailer
- ❑ sponge
- ❑ spraycover
- ❑ lock,key,cable
- ❑ PFDs
- ❑ maps/charts
- ❑ compass
- ❑ whistle
- ❑ throw bag

SHELTER
- ❑ tent & poles
- ❑ ridge pole
- ❑ tent fly & ropes
- ❑ tent pegs
- ❑ kitchen tarp
- ❑ poles & rope
- ❑ biffy tarp &
- ❑ rope & hoop
- ❑ ground sheet

TOOLS
- ❑ axe
- ❑ shovel
- ❑ saw
- ❑ small vice grips
- ❑ duct tape

- ❑ string
- ❑ work gloves
- ❑ Swiss knife
- ❑ flashlight &
- ❑ batteries, bulb
- ❑ candle
- ❑ needle & thread
- ❑ carabiners

FIRST AID KIT
- ❑ bandaids
- ❑ gauze pads
- ❑ 2" bandage
- ❑ adhesive tape
- ❑ disinfectant
- ❑ cotton batting
- ❑ tweezers
- ❑ needle
- ❑ scissors
- ❑ baking soda
- ❑ tensor bandage

PERSONAL
- ❑ toilet paper
- ❑ medications
- ❑ aspirin
- ❑ antacids
- ❑ deodorant
- ❑ soap & cloth
- ❑ towel
- ❑ hair fixin's etc.

- ❏ contact lens solution
- ❏ reading glasses
- ❏ sun glasses
- ❏ sun screen
- ❏ insect repellent
- ❏ shaving kit
- ❏ tooth brush
- ❏ tooth paste
- ❏ dental floss
- ❏ wrist watch
- ❏ mirror
- ❏ lipchap stick
- ❏ hand lotion

SLEEPING
- ❏ sleeping bag
- ❏ thermorests
- ❏ pillow case
- ❏ sleepwear

CLOTHING
- ❏ wool socks
- ❏ light socks
- ❏ light shirt
- ❏ heavy shirt
- ❏ wool sweater
- ❏ underwear
- ❏ shorts
- ❏ swimwear
- ❏ light pants
- ❏ warm pants
- ❏ nylon shell
- ❏ warm jacket
- ❏ handkerchiefs
- ❏ cap with visor
- ❏ sneakers

- ❏ hiking boots
- ❏ toque
- ❏ gloves
- ❏ mosquito net

RAINWEAR
- ❏ rain hat/parka
- ❏ rain pants
- ❏ rain parka
- ❏ waterproof boots

RECREATION
- ❏ camera & spare batteries
- ❏ film
- ❏ journal & pen
- ❏ novel
- ❏ binoculars
- ❏ music instruments
- ❏ reference books
- ❏ fishing tackle &
- ❏ fishing rod &
- ❏ permits
- ❏ lawn chairs
- ❏ day pack

KITCHEN
- ❏ stove & fuel
- ❏ matches
- ❏ nest of pots
- ❏ plates
- ❏ bowls
- ❏ mugs
- ❏ cutlery
- ❏ filleting knife
- ❏ frying pan
- ❏ lifter

- □ can opener
- □ dish towel
- □ dish cloth
- □ dish soap
- □ scrubber
- □ water container
- □ foil
- □ paper towels
- □ garbage bags
- □ ziplock bags
- □ mesh bag
- □ wood spoon
- □ fire grate

BREAKFASTS

- □ inst. oatmeal
- □ orange juice
- □ powdered milk
- □ instant coffee
- □ prunes
- □ bread
- □ butter
- □ marmalade...
- □ sugar
- □ biscuit mix
- □ syrup...

LUNCHES

- □ bread
- □ butter
- □ cheese
- □ pate'
- □ mustard
- □ oranges
- □ carrots
- □ lemonade powder

- □ beer
- □ pop

SNACKS & HAPPY HOUR

- □ hard candy
- □ gorp
- □ peanuts
- □ rum &
- □ hot chocolate
- □ beer
- □ tea &
- □ instant decaf.

DINNERS

- □ magic pantry
- □ freeze dry peas
- □ instant potatoes
- □ carrots
- □ onions
- □ cooking oil
- □ instant soups
- □ salt
- □ pepper
- □ vinegar
- □ ketchup &
- □ weiners
- □ hard sausage
- □ macaroni & cheese
- □ canned meat
- □ canned fish

- □ water &
- □ water purifier
- □ canned fruit
- □ puddings
- □ cookies

NOTES

Packing the Wilderness Camping Canoe

The rules are:
- **KEEP THE HEAVY STUFF ON THE BOTTOM AND IN THE MIDDLE,**
- **KEEP THE CANOE IN TRIM**
- **KEEP THE PROFILE LOW.**

Canoes like everything else respond to the laws of physics. The lower the center of gravity, the more stable the canoe will be. The more the weight can be concentrated toward the center as opposed to the ends of the craft, the better the canoe will respond to waves. This is the reason a solo canoe can handle rapids that would swamp a tandem canoe.

A canoe with a low profile not only looks better, but there is less surface for the wind to act on. A spray cover helps cut the windage too. A canoe in trim is evenly balanced bow and stern. A well trimmed canoe paddles more efficiently than does one down in the bow or stern. Other things to consider are the placement of containers and gear that you may have to get at quickly. We keep our rain gear, nylon shell and sweater in a waterproof soft pack stuffed under the seats. Our lunch bucket or box is stowed in front of the stern paddler where it slips out easily without having to unpack the whole canoe or take the spray cover off. Our lunch container also holds first aid items, sunscreen, insect repellent, camera, binoculars, sunglasses and any other small item we think might be needed. Our spare paddle is slipped under the spray cover where it is instantly available and where it helps to provide a peak which keeps water from pooling on the cover.

Prior to going on our canoe trips, I always have to assemble all the stuff we take and review on dry land where it all goes. This is especially important when we have a new canoe or are changing some of the containers we used before. At the put-in it might be raining, muddy or otherwise difficult and that will not be the time to start experimenting.

SPRAY COVERS

Spray covers are used by many trippers for several reasons. The first is to turn away the odd wave that breaks on the boat. The second is to keep paddlers and gear drier in the rain. A full spray cover, either one piece or three piece, also covers the paddlers making it unnecessary to don rain gear pants. A drier canoe means no bailing and more comfortable paddling. A third reason is to reduce windage, while a fourth reason is aesthetics.

The mountain of gear that six canoes pack is impressive to say the least. On our trip up the lower Stikine River we took six canoes, twelve paddlers and all our gear on two jet boats run by the Telegraph Creek Indians. It was obvious that the natives thought that we were shy a few smarts as we surmised by the quiet snickers as it was all disgorged on the Telegraph Creek beach. However, ten minutes later it was all neatly stowed away below gunnel level, spray covers were in place....and the Indians came down to take pictures!

Some trippers are content with just a cargo cover snapped in place while others just cover all of their gear with a tarp tucked down the sides and keep it in place with lacings of light rope over it. A loose tarp at the mercy of the wind makes paddling more difficult if not downright hazardous.

Headed out for a day in the drizzle. Jack Wainwright photo.

Make sure it all fits before leaving home. Jack Wainwright photo.

MAKING A SPRAY COVER

To make a cargo cover, tape nylon pack cloth over the area to be covered. Tape it in place leaving enough material down the sides to make a double one inch hem and a finished overlap of two inches. Run a piece of chalk on the outside edge of the gunnel to get the shape. Remove the cloth and sew hems all around. Install the female half of fabric snap fasteners every eight inches through the hems on the sides. Tape the finished cargo cover back on the boat and mark where the male half of the snap fasteners will be attached to the canoe with pop rivets through the hull. Make it gently taut. Hot sun will shrink pack cloth slightly. Wet pack cloth magically stretches. If it is too tight to stretch over your gear, wet it first.

A full spraycover is made the same way except that it has cockpit sleeves where the paddlers sit. The sleeves are made of lighter coated nylon and may be held in place around the waist by elastic tape or velcro. The important thing is that the sleeve must be tight enough to stay up and deflect water, and at the same time be loose enough so the paddler is not impeded if he has to make a wet exit after dumping the canoe. Full spray covers are available commercially from canoe dealers.

The spraycovers we use and describe here are for light duty. They are not designed to turn an open canoe into a closed boat. We have inadvertently tested ours a few times though and it worked fine. Once we inattentively rolled off a boulder on the North Saskatchewan River, wetting the cover a full eleven inches amidships....and we didn't ship a drop! Another time we stupidly got committed to a series of huge standing waves with holes so deep my bow paddler wife, Elise, could not get her paddle in the water....and again we didn't ship a drop.

There are commercial spray covers that are more robust. They fasten on with cables and turnbuckles and look like they could withstand any assault. The most convenient ones have a cargo hatch to let you get at your gear without taking the whole cover off.

Wilderness Canoe Camping Trips in B.C.
Circuit Trips (No Shuttle)

CLEARWATER-AZURE LAKES
- **Location:** North of Clearwater, B.C., in Wells Gray Park.
- **Difficulty:** easy trip suitable for intermediate and novice paddlers; mostly lake and fast grade I water; one portage of .5 km; no shuttle required.
- **Length:** 96 km return (106 km from Clearwater Campsite). Clearwater Lake is 21 km long from the put-in at the boat launch to the river; the river is about 3 km, half of which can be paddled upstream; then portage .5 km to Azure Lake which is 24 km long. On the return trip, the 3 km river is easily run by any paddler with any knowledge of moving water skills. Allow at least 4 days for a round trip.
- **Hazards:** The lakes can get windy and summer squalls are common but shore access is frequent. Power boaters can navigate the river and may be found on both lakes and at many campsites. Apart from fast water with some standing waves, the river is easily run.
- **Camping:** As this is in Wells Gray Park, camping is regulated. Camp only in designated sites. The present fee is $6 per canoe per night. Permits are purchased on a self register basis at the Clearwater boat launch 5 km north of Clearwater campsite. You must fill out the form and deposit the appropriate amount of cash in the strongbox. They do not accept cheques or credit cards. The park ranger may check for your receipt at anytime. There is a $500 fine for non-compliance. Dogs are no long permitted, even on a leash. There are no stores in the park. Regulations may soon ban the use of disposable containers. Check with the Parks Branch before setting up your provisions.

- **Access:** Put in and take out at the boat launch on Clearwater Lake. Park in the designated lots. As this is a return trip, no vehicle shuttle is required.
- **Maps:** The B.C. Provincial Parks issues a free map of Wells Gray Park in 1:250,000 scale (2.5 km per cm) which shows the location of designated campsites. Pick one up at the boat launch or any Parks office or Government Agent office.

  BC Parks Zone Manager, Box 70, Clearwater, B.C. ,V0E 1N0; phone: (604) 587-6150 .

  They are only open during normal business hours.

  BC Parks Regional Director, 101, 1050 West Columbia Street, Kamloops, B.C. V2C 1L2; phone (604) 371-6400 or

  BC Parks District Manager, 1210 McGill Road, Kamloops B.C. V2C 6N6; phone (604) 828-4494

  A contour map scale 1:125,000 is also available from the Parks Offices.

  The official National Topographic map scale 1:250,000 is #93-A (Quesnel Lake) but it may also need # 83-D to show the end of Azure Lake. They are not needed as the Park maps are quite adequate for this trip.

This is an easy, safe trip to start wilderness canoe camping because there are powerboaters and licenced commercial operations on the lakes to turn to should you have any emergency. Paddle close to shore to minimize the hazard of powerboat waves and to facilitate landing if winds and waves get too strong. Do keep a sharp weather eye for approaching squalls which are frequent on summer afternoons when thunder clouds are present. Do not underestimate the intensity of these squalls. They can generate breaking waves quickly. The prudent paddler will not only take shelter but will also have secured his boat. It is not uncommon for winds to blow away untied canoes.

On clear days, paddlers approaching the north end of Clearwater will spot Mt. Huntley's snowy peak to the north and from the west side of Clearwater may glimpse Azure Mountain and extinct volcanoes to the east. Ivory Creek Campsite is designated for canoeists and also hosts an eagle's nest. Watch for otters and bears, too.

For the best landing sites, stay to the east shore on Clearwater Lake and up the river channel between the lakes. Be aware that the river generates large back eddies on either side as it enters Clearwater Lake which particularly affects paddlers coming up the west shore.

Paddling up the river to the portage can be a slog requiring the ability to read water and ferry or it can be fairly easy. Generally, the best route is along the west bank about 500 m to the island. Many land there and scout as water level affects the next leg. Stay east of the island in the river and paddle up to the portage trail. The portage is on river left, which is the left bank if you were going downstream. There is a detailed map of the river at the put-in. Make note of it. The river is navigable by powerboats but like all rivers, may change or alter channels as water levels vary. Be alert.

The portage trail is a pleasant 15 minute walk to Azure Lake, but it sports a 99 step staircase, making portage wheels useless. Years ago my brother-in-law, Bill, and I took our kids on this trip. We had four canoes and seven children. The portage start was a mosquito infested bog which quickly became a short, steep trail. Even though the trail was only an easy quarter mile walk once on top, the steep start was too much for the kids to pack gear up. Bill and I would have had to haul four canoes up it too. I had brought a 5 h.p. outboard to let us avoid the portage. The idea worked fine for one canoe to run up the river, but when we lashed all four in line and paddled with the motor full out, the river was still too fast to run up. A miscue dumped one canoe and only a quick slash of a knife kept the others from getting dragged over too.

We then hailed a commercial fishing guide who was working the river and he agreed to run us and our boats and gear up to Azure Lake. From our point of view, it was $35 well spent. The trail is much improved now but the mosquitoes are as hungry as ever.

Campsites are adequate. The Osprey Campsite is reserved for canoeists and the one opposite it is the start of the hiking trail up Mt. Huntley. This hike is 12 to 16 hours. Fishing can be good. Ospreys abound. A feature not to be missed is Rainbow Falls near the end of Azure Lake. The mist from the falls encourages magnificent pillows of moss on the trees. The mountain scenery is great from either side of the lake. Paddlers can get to the far eastern end of Azure and see the pristine country that powerboaters cannot get into. Watch for moose and bears in the fall.

This area is in the interior wetbelt. The mean annual precipitation for Clearwater Lake is 100 to 150 cm while for Azure it rises to 150 to 250 cm. The average days with measurable precipitation in July is 10 to 13. This area often gets summer thunder storms that build up in the late afternoon on hot days so take your rain gear, camp tarps and plan to paddle early in the day.

Read all the information you get from the Parks and note that the river outflow at the south end of Clearwater Lake is extremely dangerous and no paddler should venture near it.

The river channel between the lakes is also fed by the Clearwater River draining Hobson Lake. This river is not navigable and should be avoided. It is a 13 km hike to Hobson Lake and there are no park campsites on it. A hike with light daypack takes 12 to 14 hours return. Airplanes are allowed to land on Hobson Lake and Clearwater Tours (674-2121, 674-3052) has a few rental canoes there.

Wells Gray wilderness. Jack Wainwright photo.

BOWRON LAKE CIRCUIT

- **Location:** Bowron Lake Provincial Park 119 km east of Quesnel, B.C.
- **Difficulty:** There are 8 kms of portaging over improved trails. Wheeled carriers can be used on all of them. The 16 km of river paddling include rapids to grade two on the Isaac R. and sweepers and deadheads on the Cariboo R. Some river experience is essential as novices frequently dump in the rivers. The rest of the 116.2 km trip is lake paddling with 1.2 km of easy lining.
- **Length:** The full circuit is 116.2 km long. Racers have done it in two days. Most people take a week to 10 days to paddle it and add a few layover days for fishing, hiking or inclement weather.
- **Hazards:** As noted above, the rivers have rapids to grade two, deadheads and sweepers. At low water, the Cariboo River may have many shallow gravel bars. Power boats and aircraft are permitted only on Bowron Lake. Bears can be a problem at campsites and portages. Winds can come up suddenly on the east and south side fjord-like lakes, especially Isaac and Lanezi.
- **Camping:** Camping is strictly in designated sites only. A campsite is located at the beginning (and end) of the trip which is sometimes forced on you due to the limit of 50 persons departing per day. Reservations are always required for group travel (7-14 people) and for all paddlers in June, July and August otherwise it is first come first served with a maximum limit of 6 people travelling together.
Firewood may not always be available or it may be big rounds. Carry a good campstove and a 3/4 or full size sharp axe. Bear caches are provided and must be used. Firearms are not allowed in Bowron Lake Provincial Park. Dogs, cats and other domestic pets are not allowed on the circuit. Garbage must be packed out.
- **Access:** All paddlers camping in Bowron Lake Park must register at the Park registration office located at road end

near the Bowron Lake Campground. At the present time the fee to do the full circuit is over $60 cash. Cheques and credit cards are not accepted. The start is a 2.4 km portage from the parking lot to Kibbee Lake. Take-out is just south of the parking lot at a very visible float at the north end of Bowron Lake. An alternate trip which avoids all portaging is to paddle the west side lakes of Bowron and Spectacle, a total of 24 km. Put-in and take-out at the float on Bowron Lake at the campsite.

•**Maps:** BC Parks provides a free map with a scale of about 1: 100,000 which shows campsites, shelters and portages. A contoured map scaled 1:63,360 is available from: MAPS B.C., Parliament Buildings, Victoria, B.C.

The Bowron Lakes circuit is well known even by non-paddlers because it is frequently the subject of television programs and outdoor publications. A geological quirk has created this unique chain of rivers and lakes that lets you put-in and take-out without shuttling vehicles. The fame of this circuit has resulted in the need for permits to regulate the number of paddlers otherwise the wilderness experience would be lost. For many of us, the present crowds are too much. We have many wilderness experiences still in B.C. where camping is unregulated and permits and fees do not apply....yet.

It is partly the paddling pressure on a few well known B.C. sites that has prompted us to publish this book. Hopefully we will spread out the paddlers all over the province and limit or delay the need for permits to paddle.

The trails have been greatly improved from the days when we slogged up to our ankles in mud but the weather has not. This area lies in the interior wet belt which gets fairly even precipitation all year round. The wetter east and south sides of the circuit can get up to 250 centimeters of precipitation....that is over eight feet! July gets on average 10 to 13 days of measurable precipitation.

As we started one trip, it had rained continually for 15 days. We met people portaging back out, quitting because weather had pinned them down too long. Yet for the next nine days, we experienced very little rain or wind although we did go down half of Isaac Lake under a makeshift sail. The rainfall nourishes good sized fir, hemlock and cedar trees.

An unmistakable observation is the size of the Bowron logging clearcut. It is said that only two of man's endeavours are visible from space. One is the Great Wall of China, the other is the Bowron Clearcut. Foresters hasten to tell us that it was insect infestation that precipitated the need for such a large clearcut and politicians like to assure us that it is now replanted and is therefore the largest tree plantation in the world.

The east side is the most scenic with snow capped mountains, green forests and lakes. Fishing is decent in any of the lakes. We did not wet a line until the portaging marathon into Isaac was over, but there we caught Kokanee in the bays and Lake Trout in deeper water. Even the clear water of Unna Lake yielded a 24 inch laker....and we are far from proficient fishers. Rainbow trout are present every-where...unless you planned to catch fish for regular meals, at which point they disappear.

Running Isaac River in a classic Greenwood. Bill Kent photo.

The Cariboo River is glacial in origin and carries a lot of glacial flour and silt which makes it quite opaque and cold. So whereas the first half of the trip has clear water, the southern stretch is silty.

The west leg of the trip is through much lower terrain through meandering streams, beaver ponds, reedy areas and lakes. Here you may have impediments or not enough water to the extent that you must push, pull or drag your canoe up Babcock Creek and over beaver dams. This is not difficult and in the summer, the warm water is a welcome change. The drier climate of the west side features Lodgepole Pine as the climax forest.

Drinking water is readily available from streams and lakes but BC Parks recommends boiling all drinking water to kill the intestinal parasite Giardi Lambia which is found all over North America and which causes Giardisis in humans. Symptoms include diarrhea and abdominal cramps. The U.S. Department of Health recommends iodine or chlorine treatment. See appendix page 227 for details on purifying water. B.C. Parks recommends boiling the water.

B.C. has an abundance of the large land mammals of North America. In Bowron Lake Park you will probably see black bears, moose, porcupines, beaver and muskrat. Grizzly bear, caribou and mountain goats inhabit the higher elevations in summer, although Grizzlies come down to feed on spawning salmon in the fall.

B.C. Parks publishes a very comprehensive brochure titled "Bowron Lake Provincial Park". It is available from B.C. Parks offices and Government Agents. For additional information contact: B.C. Parks District Manager 540 Borland Street, Williams Lake B.C. V2G 1R8 ; Telephone (604) 398 4414; FAX (604) 398 4686 or BC Parks Regional Director, 430-1011 Fourth Avenue, Prince George, B.C., V2L 3H9

Circuit distances:	Trails	Lakes	Rivers
Portage: Bowron to Kibbee Crk	2.4km		
Paddle: Kibbee Lake		2.4 km	
Portage: Kibbee Lake to Indianpoint Lake	2.0 km		
Indianpoint Lake		6.4 km	
Portage: Indianpoint Lake to Isaac Lake	1.6 km		
Paddle: Isaac Lake, west arm		6.8 km	
Paddle: Isaac Lake, main arm		31.2 km	
Paddle and Portage	1.6 km		
Isaac River: Isaac L. to McLeary L.		1.2 km	
Paddle: McLeary Lake		1.2 km	
Paddle: Cariboo R.: McLeary L. to Lanezi Lake			5.2 km
Paddle: Lanezi Lake		14.8 km	
Paddle: Cariboo River: Lanezi L. to Sandy Lake			1.2 km
Paddle: Sandy Lake		4.8 km	
Paddle: Cariboo River: Sandy L. to Babcock Creek			3.6 km

(paddle another 400 m to Unna Lake...hike to Cariboo Falls 24 meters high) **DO NOT PADDLE PAST UNNA LAKE OR YOU WILL SEE THE FALLS FROM A DIFFERENT PERSPECTIVE.**

	Trails	Lakes	Rivers
Line canoe: Babcock Creek: Cariboo River to Babcock L.	1.2 km		
Paddle: Babcock L.		2.8 km	
Portage: Babcock L. to Skoi L.	.4 km		
Paddle : Skoi Lake		.8 km	
Portage: Skoi Lake to Spectacle Lake	.4 km		
Paddle: Spectacle L. and Swan L.		12.4 km	

Paddle: Swan L. outlet

    (Spectacle L. to Bowron R.)   .4 km

Paddle: Bowron River (a slow

meandering stream) to Bowron L.   4.0 km

Paddle: Bowron Lake   7.2 km

    The Bowron Lakes Circuit is a "must do" for any B.C. paddler. Go any time from June through September. Earlier or later and you may need an icebreaker.

MURTLE LAKE

- **Location:** 26 km west of Blue River, B.C. which is on Highway 5 north of Kamloops
- **Difficulty:** Lake paddling only, but there is a 2.5 km portage from the road end to the lake on an improved trail which is now suitable for canoe carts and wheelchairs..
- **Length:** This Y- shaped lake has two arms. The west arm is the most popular and the most crowded. It is about 15 km long from the put-in. The north arm is about 24 km long from the put-in. There are over 100 km of shoreline to explore on this lake. Allow at least four days and up to a couple of weeks if you are going to try and see it all.
- **Hazards:** Wind is the biggest hazard. There are no unofficial powerboats allowed. A ranger patrols the lake but you may have difficulty contacting him in an emergency. This is a popular canoe trip, though, so there are usually other canoe campers nearby should help be needed.
- **Camping:** Camping is allowed only in designated sites which are shown on the maps you get when you purchase your camping permit. The current charge is $6 per canoe or party per night. Permits must be purchased at a shop in Blue River, B.C. Firewood is provided at designated wood lots and is not supplied at campsites. Standing trees may not be cut. Take a good camp stove and a decent sharp axe to split the firewood. Bear caches and pit toilets are provided at most campsites.
- **Access:** From Blue River take a gravel road for 27 km to a parking area just inside Wells Gray Park. The parking area

is not large and very large vehicles may have difficulty maneuvering and parking. There is no official security for vehicles, but there are always people coming and going. Camping is not permitted in the parking area. Portage 2.5 km to Murtle Lagoon which opens into Murtle lake, or carry on another 1.5 km to the lake itself and where the first campsite is. The put-in and take-out are the same place so you will have the same portage on the way back.

•**Maps:** The Provincial Parks Branch puts out a free map of Wells Gray Park in 1:250,000 scale. It shows the designated campsites and hiking trails for Murtle Lake and is adequate for canoe tripping. The Carousel (a store) in Blue River also gives a map of the area when you get your permits from them. They are open 7am to 10pm every day during the summer. The National Topographic Map for Murtle Lake is "83-D Canoe River". See page 114 for the addresses and phone numbers of Provincial Parks offices for this area.

Murtle Lake is designated as a Nature Conservancy and as such is subject to special rules. No motors of any kind are allowed. Dogs are also banned and starting in 1994, the parks branch is instituting a ban on non-burnable food and beverage containers. Firearms are prohibited. All garbage must be packed out. To avoid surprises, you may wish to call BC Parks for the latest restrictions.

Murtle Lake is an enchanting place to canoe camp. The miles of sandy beaches, interesting lagoons, good fishing, swimming and lack of any motor sounds, roads, railways or powerlines give a great wilderness experience. One of our most memorable campsites was there. It had it all plus a full moon rose in a clear night sky and the mosquitoes retired early.

Mosquitoes! The quiet stagnant lagoons breed them by the millions. The campsites can not avoid them although they are minimal on the islands. Take mosquito netting hats, lots of repellent and pray for a little breeze to keep them back in the bush.

There are hiking trails accessible only by canoe that will give you further wilderness experiences. They are well described in the Parks maps and brochures. We landed on one beach and found the largest

Spruce I've ever seen. It took all nine of us with arms outstretched to measure its girth.

Murtle Lake borders on the interior wet belt. The west end averages an annual rainfall of 100 to 150 cm while the north end averages 150 to 250 cm of precipitation per year. The average days of measurable precipitation in July range from 10 to 13. The mean July temperature is a comfortable 16 to 18° C. The elevation is 1067 m. Afternoon winds and thundercloud buildup is not uncommon on warm summer days. Watch for squalls.

All of the preceding tells you to be prepared. Rain gear, waterproof tents and tarps are a must. So are bathing suits and fishing gear. Plan to paddle early in the day to avoid the afternoon winds and co-incidently also be early to get a good campsite.

The Murtle River outflow at the west end is not navigable. There is a five km hike from Diamond Lagoon at the west end of the lake to McDougall Falls on the Murtle River.

Murtle Lake portage. Jack Wainwright photo.

NATION LAKES

- **Location:** North of Fort St. James.
- **Difficulty:** This trip is lake travel with about 16 km of moving water between the lakes. These short rivers are fairly swift in high water; slower and shallow in low water. Log jams requiring scouting and portaging are noted on the rivers between Tsayta and Indata Lakes and between Indata and Tchentlo Lakes. Sweepers are an additional hazard in high water. High water and high mosquito count are generally in June. The long shuttle and rivers can be avoided if you wish to just explore the shores of 28 km long Chuchi Lake.
- **Length:** Tsayta Lake is 20 km, then 6.5 km river, followed by 11 km Indata Lake then 4.5 km river, followed by 37 km Tchentlo Lake, then 5 km of river followed by 28 km Chuchi Lake. Plan on a long day just for the shuttle and 7 to 10 days paddling.
- **Hazards:** Apart from the log jams, the main hazard is wind and remoteness. All this plateau country gets summer storms that may build up in the late afternoon on hot days and which generate squalls on the lakes. The lakes lie in an east-west direction which allows normal east and west winds to generate good-sized swells. Lodges and cabins may or may not be occupied. Few people frequent the area so paddlers must rely on their own resources.
- **Camping**: Camping is unorganised and sites are not hard to find. BCFS has several campsites along the lakes. Firewood and drinking water are available. Practise minimal impact camping. Be especially careful not to disturb the fragile ecosystem around the hot springs.
- **Access:** To get to the take-out, from Fort St James take the gravel Germansen Landing North road for about 100 kms. Watch for a road to the left before you get to the Nation River and a sign saying Chuchi Lake. It is about 5 km farther to the lake. The abandoned Simpson Bay resort is a good landing area with road access. Leave a vehicle there or arrange for a local resident to drive you to the put-in on Tsayta Lake and bring your vehicle back.To get to a put in on Tsayta Lake, drive

north of Germansen Landing for about 90 kms, then west on
the road around Germansen Lake for 64 km, then west of
Fall-Tsayta FSR for about 20 kms to Tsayta Lake. Put in at
Tsayta Lake Lodge and leave vehicles there. There are no
services on these roads. Take lots of gas for a return trip
of about 400 km. It is a four hour drive from the take-out to the
put-in. The roads are rough. Be prepared for flat tires and even
trees down across the road in this little travelled remote chunk
of B.C. An alternative road to the put-in from Ft. St. James is
along the north side of Stuart Lake, through Pinchi Reserve,
north on Leo Creek FSR and on toward Takla Landing on the
Driftwood FSR to where it meets Fall Tsayta FSR.
   •**Maps:** Use the National Topographic System map 1:250,000
   93-N Manson River. Also get the BC Forest Service map for
   the area which shows all the roads mentioned. BCFS also
   prints a 1:100,000 recreation map of this chain of lakes
   showing log jams, FS campsites, lodges and the Tcchentlo
   Lake Hot Springs (warm, not hot).
   The Nation Lake Chain is at the upper limit of the interior plateau.
The water drains east into the Peace river system and eventually into
the Arctic ocean. The fish are those of that drainage basin and include
Arctic Grayling char and Rainbow trout. There are special quotas on
Lake Char.
   The BC Resource atlas identifies the Nation River as among the
clearest water in B.C. and second coldest with summer water
temperatures averaging 6 to 11°C . The area gets the usual summer
weather for northern B.C. averaging 10 to 13 days of measurable
precipitation in July. Much of the summer rain comes from local
storms that build up later in the day. It is not unusual to start each day
in sunshine then have it cloud over and have localized rain showers
which may or may not hit your camp. These storms also produce gusty
conditions, so canoeists are wise to paddle early, camp early and keep
a sharp weather eye on emerging conditions. The weather can be hot
with daytime highs reaching 30° or very cool.
   The area around the Nation Lakes is close to the boundary limits
for several big game species. Mule deer, moose, wolves, black bear

and grizzlies will be found. It is the upper limit for cougar and just below the lower limit for Arctic caribou and mountain goat.

The biogeoclimatic zone is similar to that of the plateau country around Prince George and Fort St. James. It is sub-boreal spruce which is basically spruce forest that has a little longer growing season than the boreal spruce forests found farther north along the Alaska Highway. This zone has 3 to 4 months of 10 degree days and no frostless season.

NITINAT LAKE AND WEST COAST TRAIL
- **Location:** Vancouver Island, south of Barkley Sound.
- **Hazards:** Wind is the main hazard, unless you also try the triangle trip which has difficult portages.
- **Length:** From the put-in at Knob Point Forestry Campsite on the north side, it is a 20 km paddle to the end where you take out at the West Coast Trail, river right. There is another road that lets you put in farther down the lake on the south side leaving you a 12 km paddle to the end. The hike to see Hole in the Wall and Tsusiat Falls is about 6.25 km, one way. This trip lends itself nicely to a three-day weekend, if you don't count the ferry time from the mainland.
- **Camping:** From the end of the lake where you stash your canoes to the unorganized camping on the West Coast Trail beach at Tsuquadra Creek is a portage of about 1.75 km so you will want to organize your gear to make it in one trip. Carry water. Call Parks Canada for permits to camp in this part of Pacific Rim National Park.
- **Access:** Take the road from Port Alberni towards Bamfield. Stay on Franklin South Main to Nitinat. Follow BCFS signs to the Knob Pt. put-in or stay on the road, cross the Nitinat River and take Carmanah Main to the BCFS campsite called Nitinat Lake. You can launch here or drive on taking Rosander Main which basically parallels the lake. T18 forks north to a put-in on the lake at Dakins Bay, near Doobah Creek leaving you a 12 km paddle to the end.
- **Maps:** The National Topographic System map 92C/NE (Nitinat

Lake) at a scale of 1:125,000 covers the whole area. Also get the BC Forestry Recreation map for Port Alberni Forest District, which shows the latest roads.

The Nitinat is another of our fjord lakes. It is so consistently windy that it has become a windsurfer mecca, and a paddler's nightmare. Paddle early in the day to minimize the wind factor. The reason for going is a chance to see and camp on the West Coast Trail at about its mid-point and to experience our unique temperate rain forest.

The take-out is marked by a buoy, river right, where the ferry takes West Coast Trail hikers across the Nitinat River at the end of the lake.

Do not paddle down the river as it is extremely hazardous where the out-flow meets the ocean swells surging upstream. Several lives have been lost there including those of kayakers. The estuary is tidal and at slack high tide the river is flat and seemingly benign. At low tide it rages out. If the wind is up too, it is virtually impassible.

An alternative trip is to paddle from Knob Point west about 5 km to a portage trail about one km west of Hobiton Creek, portage the 1.5 km into Hobiton Lake, paddle the 7.5 km down Hobiton to a very difficult 1.5 km portage into Tsusiat Lake. The portage is a poor trail over downed trees and slippery logs. Paddle Tsusiat Lake's 6.25 kms. Stash your canoes and hike another km through Salal choked wet trail to the West Coast Trail. Return the same way, or portage the 6 km to the Nitinat take-out. Do not plan to put in and paddle the ocean leg of this triangle.

West Coast scenery. Jack Wainwright photo.

POWELL FOREST CANOE ROUTE

- **Location:** Powell River, B.C.
- **Difficulty:** This trip is all lake paddling with 8 km of portaging over improved trails.
- **Length:** There are several options to travel the whole route or just part of it. The full circuit has 57.2 km of lake paddling and 8 km portaging for a total trip of 65.2 km. Allow two days of strenuous paddling and portaging to complete the circuit. If you plan to do a little exploring and fishing, a week is not unreasonable.
- **Hazards:** The main hazard is wind on these fjord-like lakes. Powell and Goat Lakes can be especially hazardous as they are reservoirs with drowned timber shorelines   and steep banks affording few landing sites and are 32 km of paddling. The portage trails are improved with frequent canoe rests but the one from Windsor Lake to Goat Lake is an 18% grade, 2.4 km downhill slog known as Cardiac Hill. The rivers linking these lakes are not canoeable as they are choked   with logs or have impassable rapids.
- **Camping:** There are designated sites at the put-in on Lois Lake, at the portage trail from Nanton to Ireland Lake and at the portage from Goat Lake. Unorganized camping is where you find it and not readily available as this is Rain Forest with heavy undergrowth. Logging roads access the lakes for RVers where campsites may also be found. There is no problem getting water or firewood, but carry stoves as campfires are banned during dry spells.
- **Access:** This route is paddled against the natural flow so that the portage on Cardiac Hill is downhill. Take the Sunshine Coast Highway 101 to Powell River. About 11km west of Saltery Bay or 3 km east of Lang Bay take the MacMillan Bloedel logging road north to Lois Lake. Take the right fork after 1 km. The put-in at Lois Lake Forest Service campsite is about 4.5 km after the fork, on the east side of the lake. Take out at Powell Lake Marina at Powell River, B.C.

This may also be done as a shuttle trip to avoid the hazards of paddling on Goat and Powell Lakes. Start at Lang Bay and take the Weldwood Logging Road north. Nanton Campsite is at about km 22; Windsor Lake is another 12 km. It is possible to put in on Windsor then paddle and portage back to Nanton Lake or to the circuit put-in on Lois Lake. See the next page for other options.

•**Shuttle:** It is only 29 km from the put-in on Lois Lake to the take-out in Powell River. There is no security for leaving vehicles at Lois Lake put-in. They would have to be left at Lang Bay or at the take-out in Powell River. Taxi service is available from Powell River. Lang Bay can also accommodate paddlers wishing to leave vehicles.

•**Maps:** Get the Powell Forest Canoe Route Map from the BC Forest Service. Use the National Topographical System maps 1:250,000 92-K Bute Inlet, 92-F Alberni. Larger scale NTS maps are also available.

The Powell Forest Canoe Route is best done counter clockwise. Starting at Lois Lake campsite paddle north following the west shore about 8.5 km to the start of the 1.7 km portage trail to Horseshoe Lake. Follow the west shore of Horseshoe northwesterly about 4.5 km to the opening into Nanton Lake due west. Paddle the 2 km across Nanton to the campsite and the start of the 2.5 km portage to Ireland Lake. Paddle the 1 km length of Ireland Lake to the .8 km portage to Dodd Lake. Follow the west side of Dodd for 7 km to its north end and the start of the .8 km portage to Windsor Lake. Paddle due north the full 2.2 km length of Windsor Lake to the start of "Cardiac Hill", the portage down to Goat Lake. This portage drops from Windsor Lake's 182 m (607 ') elevation to Goat Lake's 55 m. (183') elevation, a drop of 127 m (424) ft. over 2.4 km. The trail has switchbacks and gradients of 18 percent. There is a campsite at the Goat Lake end. The rest of the circuit to Powell River is 32 km of paddling. Starting at the Goat Lake campsite follow the south shore west for 12 km staying to your left all the way to Powell River. The Goat Lake/Powell Lake route just described is suggested as the one affording the best take-outs along the way. Inland Lake is an alternative take-out for those not wanting to paddle all of Powell. See the Forestry map for details.

Because Powell Lake is hazardous due to winds, snags and lack of landing sites, many paddlers shuttle to the end of Windsor Lake then paddle and portage back to the Lois Lake put-in. It is also possible to access this chain of lakes halfway at Nanton Lake campsite by vehicle via Weldwood's logging road north from Lang Bay. From this campsite, or the one at the south end of Dodd Lake, it is possible to explore both ways with unloaded canoes on day trips.

Lois Lake is about 12 km long and has 40 km of shoreline to be explored. Eight km long Khartoum Lake meets at the far east end of Lois Lake to give even more options to paddle with no portaging. There is logging road access from the Weldwood Road to the Khartoum Lake campsite which is 3 km from Lois Lake on the north side of Khartoum Lake.

This canoe circuit, first charted by Gerhart Tollas, became a reality in 1983 through the cooperation of MacMillan Bloedel Ltd., Weldwood of Canada, BC Forest Service and the Powell River Chamber of Commerce. The portages are improved trails with canoe rests every 400 m or wherever the planners thought a portager might want to rest, take a picture, or fish. Portages are well marked with bright orange triangles and trails are marked with blue dots.

BC Forestry campsites are provided about one day's travel apart, but it is allowable to wilderness camp anywhere along the way. Good campsites may be scarce, though, because this is, for the most part, fjord terrain where the shoreline plunges steeply into the lake. It is also coastal rain forest so the undergrowth is lush and the ground is often very wet.

Historically, this area was logged very early in the twentieth century and is now primarily second growth Fir, Hemlock and Cedar. There is much evidence of early logging methods and artifacts along the portage trails as some of them follow the old logging skid roads. On the Ireland Lake-Nanton Lake portage there is evidence of where Japanese loggers cut cedar for shingle bolts between 1930 and the time they were interned during WW II. The Dodd-Windsor portage was also a historic horse logging road in the 1900's when hand logging and horses were the only way timber was harvested. A dam was built backing up Powell Lake reservoir into Goat Lake to provide power for the Pulp Mill. The shore was not logged first and so the recreational use of these two lakes was marred by much drowned timber which has now rotted off leaving snags and deadheads which are particularly dangerous in windy conditions. The other lakes described were not flooded but also show the effects of nature and man with much forest debris on all the adjoining rivers and anywhere the windstorms have concentrated them.

Geologically, this area is part of the Coast Range that was uplifted some 130 million years ago and has since been sculpted by successive waves of glaciers from the ice ages of the last million years. The land is still rising even though the weight of these mile high piles of ice left 12,500 years ago. The glaciers carved deeply with the result that these steep-sided lakes are also deep.

Fishing has been so good in these lakes that there are now special gear and limit restrictions for the more accessible Lois and Khartoum Lakes. Gear is restricted to barbless hooks and daily limits are two trout under 40 cm and four kokanee.

This area of B.C. is known as the Sunshine Coast and for good reason. Summer temperatures are comfortable and fairly dry. July averages only 3-6 days of measurable precipitation. The average annual rainfall of 100 to 150 cm comes mostly in other seasons. This circuit is generally ice free all year but the best times to paddle are May through September as they are generally drier. June can be very wet.

Powell Forest circuit. Jack Wainwright photo.

Easy Shuttle Trips

COLUMBIA RIVER Upper
- **Location:** In the Rocky Mountain Trench; Golden B.C
- **Difficulty:** This is an easy trip with no named rapids or portages. The river braids and meanders.
- **Length:** From the put-in on Columbia Lake to the take-out at Donald Station the river wends about 235 km. Allow at least a week to paddle it.
- **Hazards**: Because the river braids and meanders, the difficulty is mostly in choosing the right channel. Novices with some knowledge of moving water should enjoy this trip.
- **Camping:** Camping is unorganized. Campsites are found on many islands and gravel bars although the river passes through a lot of marsh, too. Drinking water is readily available from side creeks.
- **Access:** The Columbia River is flanked by highway and railway so there are many points of access. The usual put-in is on Columbia Lake at one of the Provincial Parks where you will have a choice to paddle most of Columbia Lake or not. A put-in at the north end of Columbia Lake is at the mouth of Dutch Creek. A put-in on Windermere Lake is at Athalmere Bridge. Take-out is at Donald Station Bridge or anywhere the road accesses the river near there. Donald Station is the last take-out as the rest of the river has been inundated by the dam at Mica Creek which created the new reservoir of Kinbasket Lake.
- **Shuttle:** Hwys. 93 ,95 and 1 flank this river and are excellent paved roads. Arrangements to leave vehicles may be made at Canal Flats, Fairmont Hot Springs, Invermere, Golden and Donald Station. Car rentals are available in the larger centers. Best shuttle is probably to unload at the put-in, drive all vehicles to the take-out then return all the drivers in one

vehicle to be left at the put-in. Allow six hours for the shuttle. **Maps:** National Topographic System maps 1:250,000 82-J Kananaskis Lakes, 82-K Lardeau, 82-N Golden. BC Forest Service Recreation Site maps for Golden and Area and for Invermere District. BC Parks map of Provincial Parks of the Kootenays.

Study a map of B.C. and you will quickly note that there is a magnificent valley separating the Rocky Mountains from all the other ranges in B.C. This is called the Rocky Mountain Trench. It is the drainage basin and source of the two major rivers that drain the Pacific Northwest. The Fraser starts near Mount Robson and flows north, then west around the north end of the Cariboo Range. The Columbia starts at Canal Flats and also flows north around the Purcells and through the Columbia Mountains, then south in the valley between the Monashees and Selkirk ranges. A major tributary of the Columbia, the Canoe River, started near the Fraser and flowed south down the Rocky Mountain Trench. Mica Dam on the Columbia has turned this river into a reservoir now called Canoe Reach, while the Columbia which was drowned as far as Donald Station is called Columbia Reach. Together they make up Kinbasket Lake. The Columbia was again dammed at Revelstoke, creating a reservoir from there back to Mica Dam and was renamed Revelstoke Lake. At Canal Flats, the Kootenay River flows south around the Purcell Range down into Montana where it is backed up by the Libby Dam and then north into Canada and into Kootenay Lake at Creston. Kootenay Lake lies between the Purcells and the Selkirk ranges and drains into the Columbia at Castlegar.

In the 1880's W.A. Baillie-Grohman proposed a plan to control flooding on the Kootenay and increase agricultural land by digging a canal at Canal Flats that would divert Kootenay water into the Columbia. BC Hydro has proposed a similar scheme. It was completed. But when the second boat went through the locks, it got stuck. The locks were destroyed freeing it and never rebuilt.

The Rockies are relatively young mountains, being only about 50 million years old. They were actually formed from sediments laid down in an ancient sea. Marine fossils can be found in their layers of sedimentary rock. The ranges west of the Rocky Mountains are much older and flanked the ancient sea. As the Rockies rose, the drainage to the east was blocked and water built up in the trench and eventually joined up with the established drainage to the west. From Canada's Rockies down through South America's Andes the ranges of mountains rose about the same time and may be the result of the steady westward movement of the tectonic plates of these continents.

During the last ice age, glaciers covered this valley to a depth of 2400 meters. Only the highest peaks of the Rockies and Purcells avoided being rounded off. As the ice melted, it created a glacial lake that extended from Columbia Lake north to about Parson. You will paddle lakes that are the remnants of this ancient lake and if you climb the mountains, you will find the remnants of the iceage glaciers as they have still not melted completely even though the valley floor was ice free about 12,500 years ago.

Paddling down the Rocky Mountain Trench on a clear water river, bordered by bluffs, grassy hills and marshes and flanked by the magnificent Canadian Rockies must rank high in aesthetic appeal. Even though the valley is a major transportation route, the paddler can still get a wilderness experience. The area abounds in waterfowl and other water loving birds. Fishing for rainbow trout and Dolly Varden char can be good at the mouths of streams. Burbot and sturgeon may also be caught in the river.

This water is among the clearest in B.C. and also warms up to an average summer temperature of 11 to 15.4 °C. The area only gets 30 to 50 cm of precipitation annually with most of it falling in other than the summer months. June, though, can be wet. The valley is in the second driest July category for B.C. with average measurable precipitation of 3 to 9 days. Avoid paddling in flood season, which is generally May and June.

CROOKED RIVER
- **Location:** North of Prince George.
- **Difficulty:** This trip is generally Lake and grade I moving water with some sweepers and minor obstructions. There are no portages.
- **Length:** 95 km from the put-in at Summit Lake to the take-out at McLeod Lake.
- **Hazards:** The first part of the river may be blocked by beaver dams over which canoes will have to be dragged. In high water the current is faster and sweepers are present.
- **Camping:** Camping is unorganized. Near the take-out, Whiskers Provincial Park on McLeod Lake has a nice beach, boat launch and campsites. Carry drinking water.
- **Access:** From Prince George take Highway 97 north for 48 km to Summit Lake. 3.5 km north of the Summit Lake turn off, turn left onto Talus Road. Take the first right turn off Talus and drive to the Bridge crossing the Crooked River. Put in on the left side. There are several take-outs where roads meet the river. Take out at the north end of McLeod Lake where a road runs down to the Lake.
- **Shuttle:** McLeod Lake at the take-out is a settlement where private arrangements may be made to leave vehicles and perhaps run drivers back to the put-in. There is no supervision for vehicles left at the put-in.
- **Maps:** National Topographic System maps 1:250,000 93-J McLeod Lake or 1:50,000 93-J-7E, 93-J-10, 93-J-15W

The locals like to paddle the upper part of this trip in the high water conditions found in May and June. At that time the river is fast and sweepers are a definite hazard. Later in the season the lower water levels make this a safe easy family trip, although the beaver dams will have to be dragged over and shallow water may require alert paddling to choose deeper channels.

This river is of historical importance in that it was the water route linking the watersheds of the north with those draining into the Pacific. In 1806 Simon Fraser established the first post in British Columbia west of the Rockies at Trout Lake which was later renamed McLeod

Lake. It was from here that he embarked on his exploration trip down the Fraser River in 1808. For the next 150 years, until highways were built, this was the principal route to northern B.C.

From Summit Lake, the Crooked river flows north into the Pack and then into the Parsnip which flows into the Peace. The Bennett dam on the Peace at Hudson's Hope now backs water up drowning the upper Peace, the town of Finlay Forks and the lower Parsnip River. It is still possible to paddle down into the Parsnip, but the shores of what is now called Williston Reservoir were not logged prior to flooding and so are extremely hazardous with snags and debris.

As the Crooked River water drains into the Arctic Ocean via the Mackenzie River, the fish found are those of the arctic, primarily that fighting char, the arctic grayling.

KETTLE RIVER
- **Location:** Rock Creek, B.C.
- **Difficulty:** This trip is easy river paddling or floating, interspersed with easily run rapids to grade II. In summer the water is low enough to moderate the rapids. In high water,the rapids increase to grade III-plus.
- **Length:** From the put-in on the West Kettle 26 km north of Rock Creek to the take-out in Midway, the trip is 50 km long. From a put-in on the East Kettle, 30 km above Westbridge to Midway is 59 km. It is possible to paddle it in one day. Other put-ins at Westbridge or Zamora can shorten the trip.
- **Hazards:** There are short rapids to grade two at medium and low- water levels.There is a wood spillway 10 km below Ingram Creek Bridge which is well marked and will require a 30 m portage to go around. Remoteness is not a factor, but there are sweepers, snags and sandbars.
- **Camping:** Kettle Valley RA Provincial Park a few km north of Rock Creek on Hwy. 33 has full camping facilities. This trip lends itself nicely to vehicle or tent camping and just day-tripping the river with empty canoes.
- **Access:** Take Hwy. 33 north from Westbridge, B.C. for

about 17 km to put in on the West Kettle. Or from Westbridge take the road up the East fork of the Kettle for 30 km. The two forks meet at Westbridge.
Take out at the Kettle Valley RA; at Ingram Creek Bridge 4.5 km below Rock Creek or at the bridge in the settlement of Midway. Midway is on Hwy. 3, east of Rock Creek.

•**Shuttle:** The distances on this trip are short and vehicles will not have to be parked unsupervised overnight, so shuttling and parking vehicles is not a problem.

•**Maps:** Use National Topographic System Maps 1:250,000 82-E Penticton; or 1:125,000 82E-SW, 82E-SE. also get the B.C. Forest Service Recreation Sites Boundary District map.

This trip can be handled by novice paddlers with some knowledge of moving water skills. It is best run in the summer when water levels are lower. In high water, the rapids can be more than the average paddler can handle. These waters are called the clearest and cleanest swimming holes in B.C. July mean water temperatures range from 6 to 11° C., however, air temperature in summer can regularly exceed 30 °C. so in August the water is warmer. This area also has the driest summers in B.C. with less than 5 days average measurable rainfall in July.

Hwys. 33 and 3 follow the river as does the old Kettle Valley Railway line which was extended from mining and smelting towns of the Kootenays to service Okanagan Valley and went as far as Hope, B.C. It was completed in 1916 but is mostly abandoned now.

The East Kettle is good paddling throughout the summer, although local paddlers suggest that ABS boats are a must in low water. Locals say the East Kettle is the best and cleanest swimming pool in the world. Fishing is also good.

The West Kettle has rapids to grade II, sweepers and chutes. It is narrow and winding and is only runnable in very early summer as it loses too much water following a hot spell.

The West Kettle above Westbridge is not easily seen from the road. The river is small with sweepers. Active paddlers in the area do not recommend putting in above Westbridge on the West Kettle.

Below the Kettle Valley Provincial Park, the river is a grade I family and novice river with warm and clean water. Watch for bear and deer along the way.

From Midway, the river maintains its character as it loops into Washington and back into B.C. where it is accessed again at Grand Forks about 45 km from Midway.

PEACE RIVER

- **Location:** Northeast B.C. near Dawson Creek.
- **Difficulty:** This trip is suitable for novice paddlers with some knowledge of moving water skills. There are no portages.
- **Length:** 135 km in B.C. and the same in Alberta for a total trip of 275 river km (165 miles). Allow 10 days. Shuttle length is 256 km.
- **Hazards:** There is some fast water and chutes with minor standing waves. The river braids so the lead canoe should have experience in reading rivers and choosing appropriate channels. At the start, sudden releases of water from the dam might create a problem but the effect diminishes downstream.
- **Camping:** Camping is unorganized. This is a popular canoe trip so campsites are often well used and obvious. Water and firewood are easily obtained. Water released from the dam may affect water levels downstream so make sure you camp on high dry gravel bars or benches and draw your canoes well up the beach.
- **Access:** Put in at Hudson's Hope, a few km river left downstream of the Peace Canyon Dam. Take out at Taylor Landing, a day use park and boat launch, river right where the Alaska Hwy. Bridge crosses the Peace, for 100 km trip. Or paddle on to Dunvegan, Alberta and take out river left at the Historical site just past the Hwy 2 Bridge over the Peace, for a 275 km trip.
- **Shuttle:** There are services such as car rentals in Hudson's Hope. There is nothing at Dunvegan. We rented a car in Hudson Hope, drove all our vehicles to the Dunvegan take-out and returned in the rental. The return shuttle trip is about 500 km and will take six or so hours. We arranged for the

caretaker of the Historical site to keep an eye on our vehicles.

•**Maps:** You will need the 1:250,000 scale National Topographic System maps 94-A (Charlie Lake), 84-d (Clear Hills), 83-m (Grande Prarie)

The Peace River was the major route taken by early explorers and the fur brigades through the Rocky Mountains and into British Columbia. The Peace flows into the mighty Mackenzie system on its way to the Arctic. Its main tributaries in B.C., the Parsnip, Findlay and Peace drained northeast B.C. and afforded portages into the rivers draining into the Pacific Ocean. These waterways were important avenues of commerce before the highway system extended into the north country. And they have always been popular recreation areas.

Unfortunately, in an unprecedented building boom, B.C. fast-tracked the building of dams to harness the hydroelectric potential of these rivers. Impact studies were superficial if they were done at all.

We lost the upper Peace, the lower Parsnip and the Findlay when the W.A.C. Bennet Dam was constructed creating the huge Williston Reservoir. We also lost the recreation potential of the Williston Reservoir because the area was not logged first. This new Lake with drowned forests for beaches is too dangerous to boat due to snags, deadheads and blocked landing sites. The Peace Canyon Dam below it was the first one built and site "C", downstream, despite the lack of firm approvals has had much preliminary work done.

Peace River idyll. Jack Wainwright photo.

The downstream effects were devastating too as waterlevels sustaining the Athabasca region were diminished affecting the ecology there. Public mood has now changed to one of conserving what we have and it appears corporate developers will have to conform. As you canoe past site "C" visualize the river flooding the valley to near its rim. You may be one of the last to see the river bottom.

The Peace River valley is home to many of the large mammals found in B.C. and is an important winter sanctuary and feeding ground. The farms and fields of the upper benchlands of the Peace belie the wilderness experiences to be found on the valley floor.

The history of the area can be seen in passing...old trappers cabins, old trading forts... The original Fort St. John (1806-1823) was at the mouth of the Beatton River.

Rainy day paddling on the Peace River. Jack Wainwright photo.

TAKLA LAKE TO STUART LAKE

•**Location:** Northwest of Fort St. James, B.C.

•**Difficulty:** This trip is mostly Lake and grade I moving water. Tachie River has minor rapids requiring moving water skills to avoid rocks and boils. There are no portages. This trip is suitable for intermediate paddlers and novices with some knowledge of moving water skills.

•**Length:** From the put-in at Takla Landing to the take-out at Fort St. James, is a total of 190 km made up of 125 km of lake paddling and 65 km of river paddling. Allow at least ten days to paddle this route, more if you are exploring the lake shores too.

•**Hazards:** Summer thunderstorms or gusty squalls frequently develop later in the day in this part of B.C.....or they may miss you entirely. There are a few minor grade II rapids caused by rocks on the Tachie River.

•**Camping:** Camping is unorganized but there are lodges on all the Lakes. Takla and Stuart Lakes have BC Forestry campsites. Water and firewood are easily obtained.

•**Access:** From Fort St. James, drive NE on Germanson Landing North Road about 4 km. Go left at the railway crossing, onto the road to Tachie and Pinchi Indian Reserves. About ten km past Pinchi Reserve go right onto Leo Creek Forest Service Road. Drive north for 68 km then turn right onto Driftwood Forest Service Road for another 72 km. Watch for signs to Takla Landing. Put in at Takla Landing. Take out at the beach at the reconstructed Fort at Fort St. James or at the Provincial Park campground (Sowchea Bay RA) on the south end of Stuart Lake. Sowchea Bay is 16 km west of Hwy. 27 on a paved road.

•**Shuttle:** The shuttle is also about 190 km one-way mostly on gravel Forestry Service roads. Take lots of gas. Private security arrangements can be made to leave vehicles at Takla Landing and Fort St. James. There are services available in Fort St. James. Check also with the RCMP there and Parks Canada staff at the Fort for reliable off-duty personnel you might hire to drive your vehicle back from Takla Landing.

•**Maps:** Get the National Topographic System 1:250,000 scale maps 93-N Manson River, 93-K Fort Fraser. Or NTS scale 1:50,000: 93N-3, 93N-4, 93N-5, 93K-8, 93K-9, 93K-10, 93K-15. Also get the B.C. Forest Service Recreation Map for the Prince George region.

This trip is on some of the clearest water in British Columbia. Fishing is excellent for all species found in the Fraser River system. The water is on the cold side with average summer water temperatures ranging from 6 to 11° C. However, the air temperatures in June, July and August range to highs of 30° C. The mean daily temperature for July is 14 to 16 degrees. This area has also experienced frost in every month of the year!

There is an average of 10 to 13 days of measurable precipitation in July but the average monthly rainfall in June, July and August is only 5 centimeters. Most of the rain comes as a result of storms that build up later in the day. This type of storm creates gusty conditions and squalls that may hit you or that you may just see in the distance. In any case, it is prudent to travel early in the day and set up camp in the early afternoon. It is also important to keep a watchful weather-eye to anticipate emerging conditions.

Trip sequence and distances are: Takla Lake 60 km; Middle River 40 km; Trembleur Lake 20 km; Tachie River 25 km; Stuart Lake 45 km for a total of 190 km.

Takla Lake and Trembleur Lake have spectacular scenery and excellent fishing. A railway follows the east shore of Takla so paddlers go down the west shore where campsites are easily found.

Middle River is up to a km wide and for the most part has little noticeable current. It has swampy shores with lots of willow and is good wildfowl habitat, but camping sites are few and far between.

About halfway down the river at the mouth of Van Decar Creek there is a nice campsite near some abandoned trappers' cabins. From there, it is a three hour paddle to Trembleur Lake.

Trembleur Lake is beautiful and well worth exploring. The most direct route is a risky 12 km open water paddle directly across the Lake to the Tachie River outlet. The recommended crossing is to follow the west shore until the Lake narrows enough for a safe crossing.

The Tachie River has slow current for much of its 25 km length except for a few small rapids. Some maneuvering is required to avoid boils and the rocks in these rapids. The Tachie River also does not present many good campsites.

Stuart Lake has spectacular sandy beaches and lots of islands. Finding campsites is not a problem on Stuart Lake. On the east shore between Pinchi Bay and Fort St. James, Indian pictographs can be seen on the rock bluffs.

All three Lakes have commercial lodges catering to hunters and fishers and probably anyone else with a buck to spend. They also have power boats and radio contact should an emergency arise. Stuart Lake is closer to civilization and is thus more populated than the others. Indian reserves occupy some of the land along the way. Check your NTS maps and avoid the reserve land or make prior arrangements to camp on them.

This trip terminates at Fort St. James, but paddlers can continue all the way to Quesnel if they wish by taking the Stuart River/Nechako River trip to Prince George and the Fraser trip from there to Quesnel.

Put-in on Stuart Lake at Fort St. James. Jack Wainwright photo.

Intermediate Shuttle Trips

DEASE RIVER
- **Location:** Northwest B.C. near Dease Lake, B.C., Watson Lake YT., Lower Post, B.C.
- **Difficulty:** This river trip is mostly grade I with a few minor grade II rapids. On the last day, a short grade III rapid is easily portaged. Intermediate paddlers and novices with some moving water experience will enjoy this trip.
- **Length:** From Joe Irwin Lake it is 230 km by river to Lower Post on the Liard. It is another 80 km if the put-in is at Dease Lake. Allow at least eight days paddling time from Joe Irwin and two more from Dease Lake.
- **Hazards:** There are few hazards on this river. There are named rapids on some of the bends, but they are not all that obvious. We could not find the Cottonwood Rapids, for instance. The odd stump and log pile are easily avoided by alert paddlers. In high water significant hydraulics can be generated downstream of major islands. The most serious rapids are found on the last day. Four Mile Rapids are a km of gravel bars that make it difficult to find a channel. We picked our way down right of center, but ran out of water and had to walk it to deeper water. Others found a deep channel near shore, river right. River left looked shallow. I suspect this series of riffles shifts around and changes channel from time-to-time. Two Mile Rapids are a group of big boulders and bed rock that channel the river into 30 m of blind chutes and white water. It is easily scouted and portaged. Two Mile and Four Mile Rapids are named for the distance they are from the Liard River. On the Liard you must paddle or line up a km or so and then ferry across to Lower Post.
- **Camping:** Camping is unorganized. Campsites are plentiful on gravel bars and benches. Drinking water and firewood are

easily found. There are no services on this wilderness trip, and road access is difficult so it is important that paddlers be fully equipped and self contained. We had frost in mid-August.

- **Access:** We put-in at Joe Irwin Lake because there was an Esso station there where we arranged secure long-term parking for our vehicles. A recent report said they were now out of business. The RCMP detachment at Dease Lake should be able to advise regarding secure parking. It is also possible to put-in at Dease Lake. The take-out is at a boat launch ramp across the Liard River at Lower Post. Lower Post is basically an Indian Reserve now with a B.C. Forestry fire fighting base camp. We arranged to leave a shuttle vehicle at the forestry camp.

- **Shuttle**: This is a long way to drive and is interesting country to explore by RV. The circle tour is to drive the Alaska Hwy. one way and the Stewart-Cassiar the other. Our group of six vehicles and six canoes split up with half driving up to Dease Lake on Hwy. 37 and half driving the Alaska Hwy. first and leaving a vehicle at Lower Post to shuttle drivers back to their vehicles from the take-out. The drive from Lower Post to Dease Lake is 274 kms and takes about 3.5 hours, or 7 hours return. There did not appear to be good camping at the take-out. It is best to time the take-out early in the day so that the shuttle can be made in daylight.

- **Maps**: Most of the trip is on 1:250,000 NTS map 104-p (McDame) which starts at Pinetree Lake only 7 km north of Joe Irwin Lake. The missing part is on 104-I (Cry Lake) and the Dease Lake start is on 104-J (Dease Lake). NTS 1:50,000 are also available.

We did this trip in early August when the river was low enough to expose the gravel bars which make good bug-free campsites. Mosquitoes were only a problem at one grassy site that fronted a slough that bred them prolifically. The summer weather is generally reasonable. This trip pretty much lies in the rain shadow of the Coast Range and, as a result, annual precipitation is only 50 to 75 cm (20 to 30 in.). The whole of northern B.C. gets 10 to 13 days of measurable precipitation in July, and August is about the same. Thunderstorms can build up in the afternoons on hot days. At this latitude the nights are cool even if the days are warm. We had frost on the canoes one morning.

We saw bears and the tracks of a wide variety of mammals, including wolf and moose. We spotted a herd of caribou high on a ridge and a beaver swam by with a branch and proceeded to eat it beside our canoes at our first camp.

Dease Lake is near the divide where the rivers flow north to the Arctic Ocean. South of Dease Lake they flow to the Pacific. The fishing is generally good and the water is fairly clear. Arctic grayling are a fighting char easily taken by spincasting or flyfishing. A black Mepps #1 was deadly hardware. We had several meals of fish along the way.

Generally there are few signs of human activity along this river. The odd cabin apparently deteriorating back to nature, one or two with signs of life, no sign of roads, rails or powerlines all makes this a true wilderness experience. We saw a hunter in a riverboat at an access close to Cassiar, but now that the mine is closed and the town abandoned, I expect there will be even less of that. At McDame the Hudson Bay Company maintained a post. The buildings are still there at river left and across the river are the rotting remains of a schoolhouse and cabins. The cemetary shows it was active up to 1930 or so. In August, the place was glorious with wildflowers and berries. With the Cassiar mountains as backdrop, blue skies, river and flowers, the pictures we got were all worthy calendar art exhibits.

The history of this river ties in with that of the Stikine. The Dease was used as a route to the north from tidewater at the mouth of the Stikine. Gold seekers passed this way enroute to the Klondike. In 1940, heavy equipment and supplies were brought up the Stikine River, overland to Dease Lake and barged down the Dease to Lower Post where they had crews working from the middle each way constructing the Alcan Hwy. As we paddled this river, we wondered what kind of difficulties they had at some of the corners and shallow riffles although we knew it was done in high water earlier in the year.

Several years ago two large forest fires joined up and burned thousands of acres including the small town of Fireside. The Dease flows through this old burn and the fact that it is still evident underscores the slowness at which this land recovers. The trees here have a very short growing season with the result that a tree with a six inch diameter base may be 125 years old. The area is fragile. Minimum impact camping is a must.

FORT NELSON AND LIARD RIVERS
- **Location:** Northeast B.C. from Fort Nelson, B.C. to Fort Liard, NWT.
- **Difficulty:** The rivers are basically grade I, fast water with boils but no rapids. Log jams build up in places but are easily avoided. The Fraser River from Hope to Vancouver is comparable.
- **Length:** The Fort Nelson River is about 181 km long from the put-in to its confluence with the Liard River. The Liard River is about 100 km long from its junction with the Fort Nelson to the take-out at Fort Liard. The total trip is 281 river km with a shuttle of 204 km. Plan on eight days paddling, more if you want non-paddling days of rest.

Replenishing water on the Fort Nelson River. Jack Apps photo.

•**Hazards**: Once on the river, there is only one place to pull out
   early and that is where the Liard Hwy. crosses the river 100
   km downstream from the put-in. A major hazard then
   is the remoteness. The on-water hazards are minimal. At very
   high water access to landing sites is limited. The rivers flow
   fast but have no rapids. The current is only a concern when
   groups separate. The width of the rivers and the strength of the
   current make it difficult if not impossible to ferry directly
   across them. Inattentive paddlers could have a problem and end
   up in the same place as the logs which build up huge jams on
   the upstream ends of islands.
•**Camping:** Camping is unorganized. There are a few places that
   are Indian Reserve which you will want to avoid but otherwise
   the land is available to camp on. Firewood is abundant, but
   you'll need a good axe. Campsites are not too hard to find in
   medium to low water, but may be scarcer in high water.
   Landing sites on the Fort Nelson especially are often soft, boot
   sucking clay. There are many more gravel bars for camping on
   the Liard than on the Ft. Nelson. Carry drinking water as the
   silty rivers are coffee-with-cream colour and the side streams
   are the colour of black coffee. Some very small flows from the
   banks run reasonably clear so refills are obtainable. Be totally
   self contained as there are no services at all on this trip.
•**Access:** Put in at Fort Nelson where the Alaska Hwy.
   bridge crosses the Muskwa River. This is a few km
   south of Fort Nelson. There is a boat launch site there and
   enough space for several vehicles to camp overnight. We
   checked out other possible sites east of Fort Nelson, but the
   river has undercut its banks making it difficult to load and
   launch canoes. Take out river right at Fort Liard, Northwest
   Territories at the very obvious ferry and barge landing.
•**Shuttle:** As this is a one way canoe trip, it is necessary to have
   a vehicle at the take out. There are several options and over
   time they will change. Fort Nelson has a Tilden car rental. We
   arrived in Fort Nelson late in the afternoon, picked up the
   reserved rental car, camped overnight at the put-in, then made

the shuttle early the next day. In the morning we disgorged all our stuff at the put-in, drove all the vehicles to the take-out, then returned to Fort Nelson in the rental car. The rental car company ran us the few km out to the put-in, although we could have walked it. The return trip of 408 km was done in about 8 hours. There may soon be a regular bus service between Fort Nelson and Fort Liard. Check with the Fort Nelson Chamber of Commerce for options and local telephone numbers.

Other shuttle options include running one vehicle back to the put-in with the drivers, as long as the vehicles left at the take-out can carry all the canoes, gear and paddlers back to Fort Nelson. Many people will opt to return via the Mackenzie Hwy. and visit Yellowknife and Edmonton, which means vehicles will not return to Fort Nelson.

- **Parking:** Security for vehicles parked a long time is always a concern. In talking to Tilden, we got the name and phone number of a trucking firm in Fort Liard. We called them and they agreed to provide parking and security for $4 a day per vehicle. Most places in Fort Liard are near the river and easily walked to from the take-out. The RCMP have a detachment in Fort Liard and they too could provide or advise secure parking.
- **Maps:** You will need the National Topographic System maps scale 1:250,000 numbers: 94-J (Fort Nelson), 94-O (Maxhamish Lake), 94-N (Toad River), 95-B (Fort Liard).

The Fort Nelson River. Jack Wainwright photo.

The Fort Nelson and Liard Rivers drain the plateau country of Northeast British Columbia. There are no mountain ranges in sight, but it is not flat country either. The rolling hills have been altered by glaciers and show out-croppings of sedimentary strata, primarily sandstones, siltstones and conglomerates, that were deposited in Cretaceous and early Tertiary times 25 million to 140 million years ago. One spectacular water-carved cliff face is much photographed on the Fort Nelson about 25 km upstream of its confluence with the Liard. As we admired its special beauty, a pair of beavers swam around us continually slapping the water with their tails to remind us we were intruding.

Because much of the surrounding land is swampy muskeg, surface drainage is coffee-coloured. Clear water can be found at the small flows and seepage at cliff and high bank faces. Drinking water should be boiled or treated chemically to ensure potability. (see appendix for details).

A few cabins will be seen along the way....some friendly, some with fierce packs of dogs. Nelson Forks is shown on the maps as a town, but it is abandoned, rotting and overgrown. There are no towns between Fort Nelson and Fort Liard. There are winter roads that end at the river and allow vehicle access when the river and muskeg are frozen. There are also seismic trails that were cut while exploring for oil and gas. This area now produces much of the natural gas for the populated south.

We paddled this trip in late August and were concerned that the nights might be cold. Snow would not have surprised us. What did surprise us was the high temperatures we experienced. While paddling, we welcomed the breeze. In camp, we swam frequently in the rivers. If someone had suggested a swim in the very silty coffee-coloured Fort Nelson River on our arrival, we would have scoffed..."no way." Yet a few days into the trip, we needed relief from the heat and all six of us took the plunge. We each wore our one light shirt for a week. This was a good time to paddle as it turned out. The rivers were dropping from the higher rainfall in early summer and exposing the gravel bars which make good campsites. At high water, the undercut high banks would make it difficult to land or spot campsites. Mosquitoes were not a problem on the river or gravel bars.

Being civilized folks, we seldom got on the river before 9:30 a.m. so we seldom saw the indigenous large mammals. We saw several bears but they kept their distance. One swam across the Fort Nelson, landed near our camp and took off at a gallop, gravel flying.

The silty beaches held a fascinating record with countless tracks of moose, bears, wolves, caribou, fox, beaver and others we could not identify in our book on tracks. We found out later that Wood Bison have naturalized in this area and their tracks are similar to caribou so maybe we saw those too. One wolf track was the size of my out stretched hand, over 6 inches wide!....that's the size of a horse's hoof print!

From Fort Liard, float planes fly to the Nahanni. They will take you on the 208 km, hour-and-a-quarter flight, land on the river above spectacular Virginia Falls, give you time to have a picnic lunch and hike to the bottom of the falls and back and then fly a different return route. This is normally a 5 hour excursion. Unfortunately, fog above the falls precluded our landing, but we did see herds of dall sheep and interesting mountainous terrain at low altitudes.

This is a long way to drive, so all our group opted to complete the road circuit and visit the Indian villages and towns on the Mackenzie Hwy. We saw the mighty Mackenzie River, and experienced our first blackflies there. Toured Yellowknife and hiked trails on the spectacular precambrian shield that is exposed beyond Yellowknife on the Ingraham Trail. This bedrock is among the oldest known rock on earth with some dated at 3.6 billion years. Write the NWT Department of Tourism, Yellowknife, NT, X1A 2L9 for more information. Or call toll free: 1-800-661-0788.

FRASER RIVER upper (TETE JEUNE CACHE TO PENNY)

- **Location:** East of Prince George. Tete Jeune Cache is at the junction of the Yellowhead Hwy. 5 and Hwy. 16. Penny is 5 km off Hwy. 16.
- **Difficulty:** This trip is fairly fast grade I water with some minor grade II rapids on the bends. Intermediate paddlers and novices with some moving water experience will enjoy this trip.
- **Length:** This trip of about 240 km can be done comfortably in a week although we took twice that and did a lot of drifting.
- **Hazards:** Most hazards are easily skirted and therefore of little consequence for anyone with moving water skills. The few rapids are not much more than standing waves and are easily run in medium to low water. There are no portages. There is some braiding and in low water some channels may have gravel bars that may have to be walked over. Remoteness is not a factor as it is possible to walk to the road from many locations.
- **Camping:** Campsites are generally easy to find on the gravel bars at medium to low water levels. Cleared private farm lands frequently extend to the river banks yet there is also much apparent wilderness. Firewood and drinking water are easily found. As this river meanders through a lot of farm land, it would be prudent to purify any drinking water either chemically or by boiling. (see appendix for water purification details). We saw sixteen bears in our fourteen days on this trip in mid August, yet only one or two hung around long enough to get its picture taken. We did not cache our food, but as usual, we kept all food away from the sleeping area.
- **Access:** Put in river left below the old Tete Jeune Bridge which is 1 km below the Hwy. 5 crossing. There is room to camp at this put-in. Take out at Penny or at any of several locations shown on the map where the road comes close to the river. We took out at Dome Creek which is about 35 km before Penny. Many of the accesses are on private property and you will need the permission of the land owner. The best

way we found was to simply drive to the general take-out and ask a local where the best take-out was.

•**Shuttle:** Good security for vehicles at the put-in is not available, but there are motels and other commercial businesses nearby in Tete Jeune Cache where long term arrangements may be made. We unloaded all our gear at the put-in, then ran all the vehicles to the take-out where we left them at a private farm on the river. The drivers returned in one of the vehicles which was then left at Tete Jeune Cache. It is always more convenient to have your vehicles at the take-out as you can never be sure of your arrival time at trips end, or the weather or camping possibilities at the take-out. One vehicle doubled the shuttle vehicle's gear and ran them back to Tete Jeune Cache on the way home. Other possibilities might include hiring a local to return the drivers to the put-in which would have all the vehicles left at the take- out. One-way shuttle distance is only about 175 km on an excellent road.

•**Maps:** You will need the National Topographic System 1:250,000 scale maps: 83-E Mount Robson, 93-H McBride.

The Upper Fraser near McBride. Martin Kafer photo.

The Fraser River has its origins in the glaciers of Mount Robson Park in the Rockies and as a result carries the glacial flour that gives such rivers their characteristic milky appearance. The Fraser flows almost 1400 km and drains most of British Columbia's south-central region. Geologists tell us that the Rocky Mountains were uplifted some 50 million years ago and the Coast Range rose some 130 million years ago. As the land uplifted, the Fraser River took a course which, with its many tributaries, drained this vast area. It has maintained this course through the volcanic lava flows that created the interior plateaus a few million years ago and through at least four ice ages in the last million years. As the land was reshaped around it, the river continued to cut its bed and generally remained a meandering stream. The geologic action left the river with some canyons and stretches where it is still eroding bedrock. All the way along the Fraser, the old meanders can be seen as benches high and dry above the river.

This upper section of the river flows northwest. The Canadian National Railway line from Edmonton to Prince Rupert follows this valley to Prince George. Hwy. 16 also uses this valley to link Prince George with McBride and the Yellowhead Hwy.. Even so, these human intrusions do not encroach too much on the wilderness aspect of canoeing this river as campsites can be found out of sight and sound of civilization.

The first half of this trip wends past more farms as the road link with McBride has been in place for many years. The last half is less developed as that stretch of road is quite recent. There are also few services on that part of Hwy. 16. The populated areas tended to center around the railway stops as for many years that was the only link to the outside. The river was not used for commercial travel to any great extent as the canyons were too formidable.

Simon Fraser and Alexander Mackenzie used the Fraser in their explorations for the Hudson's Bay Company. Parts of the river were used by the fur traders, but the Peace was the river of choice for most early commerce. Simon Fraser canoed the length of the river from what is now Prince George, to its mouth and in the process almost lost his life. His ensuing report deterred others. Alexander Mackenzie used the Peace and entered the Fraser via the McGregor 100 km upstream from Prince George. The Overlanders, a group of settlers from Fort Garry (now Winnipeg), arrived at Tete Jeune on August 21, 1862. The group split, with some going south through Thompson River country and the larger group taking the Fraser where one drowned in the Fraser's Grand Canyon between Penny and Prince George.

At km 45 below Tete Jeune Cache, the river is crossed by a small bridge at Dunster. At McBride, km 85, a modern bridge takes Hwy. 16 across the river. McBride is a large town with services. You could even hike in to town and dine out. Goat River flows in at km 135 and the Goat River Rapids are passed a few miles downstream. Sternwheelers ran this stretch of river for two years until the railway bridge went in at Dome Creek blocking their route. The rapids were significant to the sternwheelers, but to canoeists they are of little concern. There are habitations and a small sawmill at Crescent Spur, km 151. Dome Creek is at km 208 and is where we took out. Penny is a railway town on river right at km 240 with road access to Hwy. 16 river left. Penny is as far as paddlers should go as the Grand Canyon of the Fraser starts soon after at km 280.

Voyageurs on the Upper Fraser. Cooper Graphics photo.

FRASER River upper (Penny to Quesnel)
   •**Location:** Northeast of Prince George.
   •**Difficulty:** Above Prince George, at medium to low water the
      river is grade I, with two km of grade II consisting of standing
      waves and rocks which will require maneuvering skills.
      Below Prince George there are two canyons and rapids
      with up to grade IV water. Do not paddle in high water
      season of May to mid-July. The first section is easier. The
      second section is for advanced and intermediate paddlers with
      good moving water skills.
   •**Length:** The river is usually run from Limestone Creek which
      is about 170 km below the Grand Canyon, to Prince
      George 90 km downstream and from there to Quesnel
      another 150 km for a total trip of 240 km. Allow two days
      paddling time to Prince George and another three
      days to Quesnel.
   •**Hazards:** Rock gardens as noted; strong hydraulics such as
      boils, powerful eddy lines and whirlpools.
   •**Camping:** Camping is unorganized. At medium to low water,
      campsites are more available. Firewood and drinking water are
      easily found. It is possible to vehicle camp each night and do
      this run with unloaded canoes. Logging roads access the river
      at several places. Get the BC Forestry Service Campsite map
      for the Prince George and Quesnel areas to locate appropriate
      roads and campsites.
   •**Access:** To put in from Prince George, drive north on Hwy. 97.
      Two km past the Huble Farm turn-off, turn right onto
      the North Fraser Forest access road and drive 37 km.
      Just past 37 km and before the Limestone Creek Bridge, there
      is an open area with a gravel bank leading to the river. Take
      out at Fort George Park or at Cottonwood Island Park at the
      confluence of the Fraser and Nechako Rivers in Prince George.
      You can also take out downstream at several locations easily
      located on the map or take out at river left in Quesnel at the
      park just upstream of the confluence with the Quesnel River.
   •**Shuttle:** Prince George and Quesnel are major population

centers with many services. It is possible to rent cars or hire taxis to help complete a shuttle. It is also possible to vehicle-camp every night if you have non-paddlers or extra paddlers who drive one day and paddle the next. It is not recommended that you leave a vehicle unattended overnight in the bush.

•**Maps:** You will need the National Topographic maps 1:250,000 scale 93-J McLeod lake, 93-G Prince George, 93-B Quesnel. Scale 1:50,000 are also available. Also get the free BC Forest Service Campsite maps for Prince George and Quesnel areas.

The Grand Canyon of the Fraser is two narrow cuts through volcanic rock that constricts the river creating rapids to grade V intensity. Many lives have been lost in this 10 km stretch of river. Below the canyon the river is again grade I but access is difficult and shuttling is time consuming so it is not described. Get on the river next at the Limestone Creek access for a 90 km trip to Prince George. At the 30 km mark you reach the Huble Farm and the Giscome Rapids 3 km downstream. This part of the Fraser was run historically and Huble farm marks a portage. This goes into the Crooked River and the Peace River system and is called Giscome Portage. However, canoeists with moving water skills can easily thread the 2 km of rock garden. This part of the Fraser otherwise is a wide float to Prince George.

Upper Fraser fur trader reenactment. Dave McCulloch photo.

The Northwest Brigade Canoe Club in Prince George is the recognized authority for paddling knowledge in this area. They have published a Canoe and Kayak trip guide for the central interior of B.C. which we have used to confirm the following: Below Prince George paddlers must be expert to intermediate with good moving water skills. Do not run this in high water. At km 26 below Prince George, the Fort George Canyon starts (also called Red Rock Canyon). It is marked by a large island mid-stream. A few standing waves announce the start of the canyon. Stay river left. Take the left channel the whole way, avoiding hydraulics by adjusting right or left sides of the left channel. We did this in 26' Brigade canoes when we re-enacted the Fur Brigade route for Parks Canada's centennial in 1985. The crews played in the hydraulics and, as I recall, dumped at least one canoe there.

The next set of major rapids come up 90 km downstream at Cottonwood Canyon. These rapids are located 5 km upstream of the confluence of the Cottonwood River and can be up to grade IV depending on water levels. The NWBCC notes waves may reach 2m in high water. At medium and low water, the preferred route is right down the middle. The rest of the trip to Quesnel is grade I water.

This part of the river was first paddled by Alexander Mackenzie in 1793. In 1993 the Sea-to-Sea Voyageur from Lakehead University along with 10 B.C. Brigade Voyageur canoes reenacted and paddled Mackenzie's historic route as the first European to cross the continent north of Mexico.

Brigade canoe, Upper Fraser. Dave McCulloch photo.

KOOTENAY RIVER (Gibraltar to Wardner)

- **Location:** Southeast B.C. Canal Flats, B.C.
- **Difficulty:** This part of the river is mostly fast water with clear or easily paddled channels, with at least one rapid to grade III on the last day.
- **Length:** From the put-in at the Kootenay Bridge above Gibraltar Rock to the take-out at Wardner, the river meanders about 132 km. Allow at least three days to paddle it.
- **Hazards**: Snags, deadheads and sweepers with a few easily run rapids and one grade III rapid where the St. Mary's River enters. Scout it and run or portage river left.
- **Camping:** Camping is unorganized. Wilderness campsites can be found . As well, roads parallel the river allowing vehicle camping and daytripping with unloaded canoes. There are BC Forestry public campsites in the area, but none on the river.
- **Access:** From Canal Flats, go east on Kootenay River Road, which follows the river, for about 27 km to Gibraltar Rock. Put-in at the bridge about 5 km upstream of Gibraltar Rock. Take-out at km 27, the Hwy. bridge at Canal Flats; at km 69 Skookumchuck, Hwy 93/95 bridge; at km 89, Wasa; at km 107, Fort Steele; or at trips end at Wardner. Take out also at informal accesses where unofficial roads meet the river. Much of the river has road access on both sides. See the BC Forestry map "Invermere" and "Southeastern BC".
- **Shuttle:** Secure parking can be arranged at most of the take-outs, but not at Gibraltar Rock. For daytrips and vehicle camping, vehicles can be left at the take-outs for the daylight hours you will be on the river.
- **Maps:** Use the National Topographic Survey maps 1:250,000 scale 82-G Fernie and 82-J Kananaskis Lakes. Larger scale NTS maps are available and give better detail. Also get the free BC Forest Service Recreation Site maps for Invermere (scale 1:250,000) and Southeastern B.C. (scale 1:300,000).

The section from the bridge above Gibraltar to Canal Flats has grade II rapids although none of them are particularly difficult. Intermediate paddlers with moving water skills will have no difficulty.

Below Canal Flats, it is a pleasant paddle through a rural landscape.

This is a silty river, but one of the warmest in the province. Average summer temperature for the river below Canal Flats is 15.5 to 20° C. For other general details of the area see the Columbia River (upper) on page 127.

Expert paddlers may wish to day trip the Kootenay River above the Gibraltar Rock put-in. Access the river at the bridge about 37 km farther along the road, just at the southeast corner of Kootenay National Park. The river is runnable at moderate water levels and will have grade III rapids. Allow for one long day of paddling this section. BC Forestry suggests this section has the Kootenay region's best wild river qualities and the most scenic features.

McGREGOR RIVER

- **Location:** East of Prince George.
- **Difficulty:** This run is mostly fast grade I with up to grade II areas in the 6 km long canyon. There is no portage around the canyon. Dave McCulloch, who organized the B.C. Rendezvous with the Canada Sea-to-Sea re-enactment, says they took this section off the itinerary as it can be tricky. High water can occur at any time on this river.
- **Length:** From the put-in at Herrick Creek to the Fraser River is 73 km. Allow two days to paddle it.
- **Hazards:** The water is fast, cold and turbid. The river reacts dramatically to local rainfall patterns. There are few access points. The canyon has navigable grade II rapids at low water and waves to 1.5 m at high water. Do not paddle it in high water.
- **Camping:** Camping is unorganized. Campsites are readily found at logging accesses and gravel bars.
- **Access:** Go east on Hwy. 16, 14.5 km from the Yellowhead Bridge out of Prince George. Turn left onto the Upper Fraser Road. Continue until 8 km past Upper Fraser, then turn left to cross the Fraser on the Hansard Railway Bridge. Go 1.5 km through McGregor Camp to the junction of Church and Pass Lake Roads. Take Pass Lake Road, pass Pass

Lake, cross the McGregor River on the suspension bridge over its impassible upper canyon. Take the next left, Logan Road, and continue until Herrick Creek becomes visible on your left. Herrick Creek is a good sized river. To get to the take-out, go back to the Church Road/Pass Road junction. Take Church Road (North Fraser Road) for about 20 km until you come to a bridge over the McGregor. Best take out is river left above the bridge.

•**Maps:** National Topographic System maps scale 1:250,000...93-I (Monkman Pass) 1:50,000 are also available. The B.C. Forestry Recreation map for Prince George will be helpful too.

This river is of historical significance as both Alexander Mackenzie and Simon Fraser used it to access the Fraser River system flowing to the Pacific Ocean from the Arctic bound Peace River system. Large parts of these rivers are the same today as they were 200 years ago when these first Europeans arrived. To paddle Mackenzie's route of 1793, put in at Herrick Creek and take out at Quesnel on the Fraser. See the Fraser River -upper (Penny to Quesnel) for the Fraser part of Mackenzie's trip.

From Quesnel, Mackenzie went up the Carrier Indian trail along the Blackwater (West Road River), down the Bella Coola River to tidewater, then 74 km down a fjord to Mackenzie Rock where he wrote in vermillion and grease: *Alexander Mackenzie, from Canada, by land the twenty-second of July, one thousand seven hundred and ninety three.*

Mackenzie's epic journey was done in a single 28 foot birch bark brigade canoe with a crew of French Canadian Voyageurs and Native guides. In 1993, brigade canoes from all over B.C. rendezvoused at Herrick Creek with three Canada Sea-to-Sea brigade canoes which were re-enacting Mackenzie's four-year sojourn across Canada and to the Arctic. Another section of this route you can still experience is the Peace River (see page 133).

NECHAKO RIVER

- **Location:** Vanderhoof, B.C.
- **Difficulty:** This upper section of river has a few rapids, perhaps to grade III at some water levels, but they are canoeable by intermediate paddlers with moving water skills.
- **Length:** Total length of this trip from the put-in 16 km below the Kenny Dam to the Stuart River is 135 km. Take out at Fort Fraser km 65; Vanderhoof km 115; Finmore km 131 or continue on down the Nechako to Prince George (see Stuart Nechako trip for details) Plan on four days paddling.
- **Hazards:** Most of the trip is just fast grade I water, but there are two grade II rapids on the first day and another below Vanderhoof. All are runable, but require scouting. The most serious hazard may be a lack of water as the Kenny Dam has reduced the Nechako's volume by 90 percent and may reverse the total upper flow into the reservoir feeding the Kemano generators. Tributaries below the dam still ensure some water in the Nechako.
- **Camping:** Camping is possible at BC Forest sites otherwise it is unorganized canoe camping. The river starts in forested country then passes large ranches in cattle country, even so, the paddler gets a lot of wilderness experiences along the way.
- **Access:** Drive toward Kenny Dam from Vanderhoof. Put in 80 km from Vanderhoof or 16 km below the Kenny Dam at a BC Forestry campsite river right. River boats launch here too. Take out at any of the road bridges downstream.
- **Shuttle:** As there is no supervision for vehicles left at the put-in and as it is always more convenient to have your vehicles there at trips end, plan on dumping all your gear at the put-in, driving all the vehicles to the take-out and either returning the drivers in one car or hiring a local to return the drivers to the put-in. Services are available in Fort Fraser and Vanderhoof.

•**Maps:** Use the National Topographic Series maps 1:250,000
93-F Nechako River, 92-G Fort Fraser, 92-G Prince George.
BC Parks map for Northern BC, BC Forestry maps for the
area.

The summer turbidity of the Nechako is listed as among the lowest in B.C. and its water temperature is among the highest with average summer temperatures of 15.5 to 20° C. The summer rainfall is a little drier than northern B.C., averaging 6 to 9 days measurable precipitation in July. Summer temperatures are the same as Prince George with mean daily July temperatures of 15 degrees and highs frequently hitting 30. The area can also have lows below zero in any month. This is a fairly dry area as annual rainfall ranges from only 30 to 50 cm.

The Nechako flows through the interior plateau which was built up by lava flows over the last 25 million years. Older granitic rock intrusions estimated at 140 to 230 million years old have been exposed by the action of iceage glaciers which reached a depth of 2300 m in this part of B.C. The lower half of the Nechako was a part of a huge lake as the ice melted.

Fishing can be good but there are special restrictions on closures, limits, and bait. In this wild part of B.C., campers may see any of the big and small land mammals of North America, or at least see their tracks and scats. Near Vanderhoof, you pass by a migratory wildfowl sanctuary.

The Nechako was called the Big River by the Carrier Indians and was a major transportation route before roads and railways accessed the area. Simon Fraser used it in 1805 as he set up trading posts. Now Hwy. 16 follows the lower Nechako from Prince George towards Prince Rupert on the coast. CN Rail does too.

The interior plateaus, with their abundant natural meadows and light forest, have always been attractive to ranchers. One of the first into the Nechako was Rich Hobson who established River Ranch not far below the put-in and wrote of his experiences. His books *Grass Beyond the Mountains, Nothing Too Good for a Cowboy,* and *Rancher Takes a Wife* are classic stories of life in early B.C.

SLOCAN RIVER

- **Location:** West of Nelson, B.C. on Hwy. 6; Slocan, B.C.
- **Difficulty:** This short river is generally grade II with obstructions caused by rocks and snags. There are no portages required. It is best done as a daytrip with empty canoes.
- **Length:** From the put-in at Slocan City to the take-out at Crescent Valley is approximately 46 km. For a shorter trip take out at the Passmore Bridge at the halfway mark.
- **Hazards:** We were told by locals that there was a bad logjam requiring a portage above Applegate. More recent information tells us this logjamb at Lemon Creek is now gone so it is possible to paddle from Slocan City. At the lower water level we had, all the corners were grade II and there was a bit of braiding where you could run out of water. Sweepers and deadheads were additional hazards. Below Crescent Valley there is 500 m of continuous Grade III which is not suitable for intermediate paddlers.
- **Camping:** There are no public campsites but there are several private campsites off Hwy. 6. From what we saw canoeing this river, there is little opportunity to wilderness camp. Check the B.C. Accommodations Guide for current campsites.
- **Access:** From Nelson, go west on Hwy. 3A/6 to Shoreacres at the mouth of the Slocan. To put in, go north on Hwy. 6 towards Slocan and Nakusp. Access the river at any of the bridges which are all west of the highway at Appledale, Winlaw, Vallican, Passmore or Crescent Valley. Winlaw Bridge marks the start of Winlaw rapids. Take out at Crescent Valley Bridge.
- **Shuttle:** We found it best to do this river as a daytrip so parking a vehicle overnight is not a concern. There appeared to be enough parking at the bridges for one or two vehicles.
- **Maps:** The National Topographic System map scale 1:250,000 is 82-F Nelson. The free BC Forest Service Recreation Sites map is 1:300,000. Get the one for Lower Arrow and Kootenay Lakes Area.

We did this short river as a daytrip in August along with several others in the Kootenays. We put in at the bridge above Appledale and took out at Passmore. The river requires paddlers with good moving water skills. At high water it might be too technical for most open boat paddlers.

The section from Slocan City to Appledale, now that the logjamb is gone, is also an easy day trip. The put-in is at the bridge one km south of Slocan City, or start at the lake.

There is a bird sanctuary on a low island ringed by waterlillies. The peaks at Valhalla Park are visible. There are a couple of minor grade I-plus rapids in this upper half of the river. The massive logjamb that was below Lemon Creek for many years is now gone, but paddlers must still be alert for remnants of it. At several places between Slocan City and Cresent Valley, long lines of old pilings, some just below the surface, are a legacy from logging activity almost a century ago.

Like much of southern B.C. this area gets an average of 6 to 9 days measurable precipitation in July. June, July and August are the driest months and high temperatures can regularly exceed 30° C. The mean daily temperature in July is 18 to 20° C. Summer water temperature is the second warmest in B.C. at 11 to 16 ° C and turbidity is the lowest, which means it is clear water.

The bedrock exposed by the river is generally metamorphic schists and gneisses of undetermined age. The last iceage glaciers covered this valley to a depth of 2300 meters and receded only some 12,500 years ago. Only the very tops of the highest mountains in this area were not scoured by glaciers.

NORTH THOMPSON RIVER

- **Location:** North of Kamloops, BC.
- **Difficulty:** This trip is mostly grade I moving water with one grade II rapid which is easily run by novices with some moving water skills.
- **Length:** From the put-in at the campsite between Little Fort and Clearwater to the take-out at Kamloops, the trip is about 130 km. Allow at least three days of paddling time.
- **Hazards:** At low water, parts above Little Fort may make choosing a deep enough channel a challenge. At higher water, a fast stretch near Barrier called Fishtrap rapids may become grade II. At Heffley an S- bend in the river always produces a grade II or almost grade III rapid. This stretch of fast water with standing waves and some boulders is a km or two long, but it is very forgiving as there is ample time to rescue and be rescued at the bottom. Many novice paddlers have been baptized and learned river skills quickly at the Heffley rapids.
- **Camping:** The put-in at Thompson River Provincial Park has vehicle and tent sites. The rest of the trip is unorganized camping on river bars and wilderness bench lands. Carry water for this short trip or purify any water picked up along the way. There is a spring piped and running into the river south of Little Fort, river right. Firewood is easily found, but carry stoves as campfires may be banned during dry spells. Travel self-contained as you would for a remote wilderness trip.
- **Access:** The put-in is usually the Thompson River Provincial Park. An alternative put-in for a shorter trip is at the Little Fort Ferry. In both cases arrangements may be made locally for secure long term parking. Our usual take-out is river left below Heffley where a road ends at the river. There is no long term parking there and the residents are not too happy with vehicles parked even while we are with them. We take-out there because Harvey Fraser, a pioneer in organized canoeing, lets us park at his home and comes down to help with our

shuttle. It is possible to paddle down to Kamloops and take out at Riverside Park. Kamloops is a major city with both car rentals and taxis available.

•**Maps:** Get the National Topographic System maps, scale 1:250,000; 92-P Bonaparte River; 92-I Ashcroft.

The Dogwood Canoe Club has for years run this North Thompson River trip on the October Thanksgiving weekend. The weather then is usually nice, the leaves are all in fall colours and the evenings and mornings crisp.

The North Thompson River was explored by fur traders 1811 to 1813. In 1862 the party of Overlanders, settlers coming in from Fort Garry, (now Winnipeg) had split at Tete Jeune Cache with the smaller group heading down this river. The upper part of the N. Thompson has several big rapids and they met with enough disasters that many opted to walk the rest of the way. Ironically, this trip, the easiest part of the river route, lay ahead of them.

Geologically, the river flows over and past rock out-croppings primarily of sedimentary rock dated at 230,000 to 570,000 years ago. This places this rock in the Paleozoic era which is the time that the first fossil records of life appear on earth. Glacial striations show that ice age glaciers flowed south down the valley. The lower third of the N. Thompson was an arm of a long ancient glacial lake that existed after the last ice age about 12,500 years ago. This lake had arms that also encompassed the Thompson, Nicola, South Thompson, Shuswap and Okanagan Lake.

Thompson River camp. Martin Kafer photo.

The N. Thompson annual rainfall is only 40 cm (16 in.). The mean daily temperature in July is 18-20° C. It can get quite hot. Thunderstorms often develop in the afternoon on hot summer days. The number of days with measurable precipitation in July is 6 to 9. The fall days of late September and early October can be especially nice. The aspens turn gold and create calendar art pictures with the contrasting dark green conifers and blue skies. Add the morning mist rising off the river following a frosty night and you have the recipe for classic pictures.

Although a highway and a railway also use this valley and it is ranching land, this river trip is still a wilderness experience. Wildlife is present but not often seen although on a recent trip, a startled bear galloped through our lunch-stop site so fast we hardly had time to snap a picture. Yes, bears do gallop, spraying gravel everywhere. Mule deer are also common.

STIKINE RIVER - Lower (Telegraph Creek to Wrangell, Alaska)
- **Location:** North of Smithers, B.C, and west of Hwy. 37 (Stewart-Cassiar)
- **Difficulty:** This is a large volume river that moves along quickly, yet it does not have any significant rapids. There is some braiding and gravel shoals but alert paddlers with basic moving water skills should have no trouble. In recent years, high water has caused erosion resulting in sweeper hazards in the middle section which require alertness and quick route changes.
- **Length:** It is 252 km (157 mi.) from Telegraph Creek, B.C. to Wrangell, AK. Allow 8 full days for paddling. The current slows appreciably after the BC/AK border.
- **Hazards:** There are no services on this remote wilderness river. River hazards are the usual gravel bars where the river braids. The rapids and canyons named on the NTS maps were significant to the sternwheelers heading to the gold fields, but are easily skirted by canoeists heading downstream. Grizzly bears and black bears fish for spawning salmon in season, but whereas most groups sight bears, we have yet to hear of a

serious encounter on this popular trip.

- **Camping:** Unorganized campsites on dry benches and gravel bars are readily available on the first 192 km Canadian section. Firewood and drinking water are easily found. On the 60 km American section, take-outs are hard to find as the vegetation grows into the water like a mangrove swamp. This is part of the Tongass National Forest and camping is organized. The US Forest Service provides cabins for a fee. Write them for maps and fee scales. It is necessary to reserve them in advance. We booked W-2 at Shakes Slough and W-12 at Garnet Ledge. We only used W-2 and as a result arrived at Wrangell a day early. That was a mistake as the Hotel was all booked up in Wrangell and we ended up sleeping on the floor of the Longshoremen's Union Hall.

- **Access:** Put-in at Telegraph Creek at the boat launch and take out at Wrangell Alaska at the small boat dock.

- **Shuttle:** It is possible to drive to Telegraph Creek which is 120 km (75 mi.) west of Hwy. 37. It is possible to fly in from Smithers or Dease Lake or Prince Rupert. It is possible to take a jet boat up from Wrangell to Telegraph Creek. At the Wrangell take-out, access is by ferry to Prince Rupert or fly out. After much research and crunching of figures, we chartered two jet boats operated by Francis Gleason of Telegraph Creek to transport our six canoes, 12 people and all our gear from Wrangell to the put-in. The trip up was delayed by fog, but at 60 km an hour we easily made it in one day. We even had supper at the Telegraph Creek Cafe before heading a few miles downstream to a first night camp. To get to Wrangell, we walked on the Alaska Ferry at Prince Rupert...which was some portage with all our gear. Reservations are essential for the ferry. We returned the same way. We also learned that the most comfortable way to sleep on those ferries is to migrate to the top deck sun lounge with sleeping bags.

- **Customs:** As this is an international trip, it is necessary to go through customs prior to boarding the Alaska Ferry. They asked if we had citrus fruit and one honest person said "yes" and had to go through her food packages to prove they were Sunkist. The rifle we carried was waved through with no permits required....you figure it. We also reported in to Canada Customs at Boundary House on the river on the way back and phoned US customs from Wrangell when we took out. As I recall, the Indians running the jet boats ignored them all.

•**Parking:** Prince Rupert is a city, so finding secure long term parking is not a problem. Taxis will run drivers to and from the parking lot. We had a shipping executive in our group who arranged parking in a company lot which was within walking distance. Call RCMP in Telegraph Creek to get advice on long term secure parking there. Expect to pay a few dollars per day per vehicle.

•**Maps:** Use The National Topographic Service maps for the Canadian part. You will need the 1:250,000 scale 104-J Dease Lake, 104-G Telegraph Creek, 104-B Iskut River. For the US part get the Marine Chart for the Wrangell area as it shows channel depths and navigation lights. The mouth of the Stikine is extremely shallow with only 2m deep water in the channel. Stay river left, close to shore. For camping, get the US Forest Service map for the Tongass National Forest.

We walked on the ferry at Prince Rupert. Our gear was heaped in a corner and the canoes were slipped under the big trucks at no charge, but any time the trucks moved, we had to be there to get them out of harms way. The ferry to Wrangell also stops long enough at Ketchikan to let tourists see the town and browse for souvenirs. We had reserved rooms at the hotel where we could also secure our gear. Canoes were locked together outside. In the morning we met our Jet Boats and zoomed up to the put-in 157 mi. upstream. The scenery was fantastic on that sunny day. At one point it is possible to see 21 glaciers. Unfortunately, that was a generally wet summer and what we saw on the way up was for the most part obscured on the way back.

Part of the fun in wilderness camping is finding good campsites. There are lots of them so we won't elaborate, but there are a couple of things that should not be missed. At the 169 km point river left just below two side-by-side islands and directly across from Great Glacier there is a warm springs creek. The water is warm, but there is no campsite there. Camp river right about km 172 at the river outlet from Great Glacier. We spent two days there resting and exploring. It is an easy walk to the glacier.

Once into the American section, keep river right and in four km from the border, head up the slough-like Kitili River for about 6 km to where a yellow water creek comes in from the right. Paddle up this creek, which is big enough for power boats too, for .5 km. From there a short trail leads to the Chief Shakes Hot Springs. Take bathing suits as many people use this free resource developed by the U.S. Forest Service. From there it is about 6 km to Cabin W2. Once into the Stikine Estuary, it is imperative that you stay river left. The channel is very close to the left shore. The very shallow mudflats of the mouth can strand a canoe on a falling tide and wind will make it extremely dangerous to be anywhere but in the channel. This area also experiences dense summer fogs. Our trip up was delayed until the fog lifted enough to see the channel markers and on our return we had the compasses out as the landmarks were obscured by fog.

This section of the Stikine River has a surprisingly long history. The local Tahltan Indian band at Telegraph Creek believes their ancestors arrived some 10,000 years ago, which would be not long after the last ice age released its grip on this land.

The Russian American Company of fur traders established a post at the present site of Wrangell in the early 1800s. Canadian and American posts were also established, but the coastal Tlingit Indians controlled the inland trading with the Tahltans. In 1867, Russia sold Alaska to the United States. Canada and the States squabbled for the next 50 years over the location of the boundary.

In 1861, gold was discovered at Glenora near Telegraph Creek. Glenora is still on the NTS map but the land has reclaimed the town. This find prompted B.C. to name it Stikine Territory and include it as part of B.C. in 1863. In 1864 an American entrepreneur persuaded Western Union Telegraph Company to finance a line to Europe from California, north through B.C. and Alaska and across Russia. It was abandoned in 1866 when the competing transatlantic cable was laid. By then the line had been built as far as present day Hazelton, B.C.. Tons of insulators, wire and other materials had been shipped to a site on the Stikine they called Telegraph Creek where they were subsequently abandoned. Forty years later, the Canadian Government used the old line to link Quesnel, Hazelton, Telegraph Creek, Atlin, Whitehorse and Dawson City.

Gold seekers again used the Stikine in 1873 for the Cassiar rush and in 1898 as an all-Canadian trail to the Klondike. Railways were planned and abandoned as uneconomical. There was regular boat service of one sort or another from Wrangell to Telegraph Creek from 1910 to 1971. In 1940, heavy machinery and supplies were shipped up the Stikine to Telegraph Creek, overland to Dease Lake, then down the Dease to Lower Post where work was progressing from the middle both ways on the Alcan Hwy. The river has only ever seen flashes of fame and has always been reclaimed by the wilderness.

The next assault came during the rush to develop hydro electric power. The Stikine and a major tributary, the Iskut were the scene of much activity as engineers laid plans for five dams and reservoirs. The Grand Canyon of the Stikine had a dam planned at site Zed that would have flooded the river inundating Hwy. 37. All these plans are on hold now as the need for electricity fell short of estimates and the new wave of power smart conservation is helping to keep them there.

The Grand Canyon of the Stikine starts near Hwy 37 and ends near Telegraph Creek. It rivals anything else in North America. It has sheer walls rising 360 m (1200 ft.). Through this 84 km long canyon the Stikine displays incredible hydraulics. At its end, the whole river is constricted to an incredible 2 m gap (6.5 ft.) . No one has ever run it and lived, with one exception. Paddlers in Prince George who read this manuscript in draft form said that they thought two or three others have done it since.

Goldcrest Productions, an English movie company assembled a team of professional rafters and kayakers so they could film the first successful descent through the canyon. They had helicopter support that videotaped the river for preview by the paddlers and whisked them and their craft out each night. It was considered run if they started where they had taken out the day before and portages were done by the paddlers. The low water that September 1985 helped them, too. Even so, the kayakers had to use rock climbing skills to portage and claim the first descent. The Grand Canyon of the Stikine is not a recommended trip.

STUART/NECHAKO RIVERS
- **Location:** Fort St. James to Prince George.
- **Difficulty:** This trip is mostly grade I with parts almost currentless and a few rapids of grade II and II-plus depending on water levels.
- **Length:** The Stuart River from Fort St. James to its confluence with the Nechako is 107 km. The Nechako from the Stuart to the take-out at Prince George is about 90 km. Allow for at least five paddling days.
- **Hazards:** Rapids to grade II and approaching grade III in low water and grade II with sweepers on several bends.
- **Camping:** Camping is unorganized and campsites are plentiful except near the more populated areas of Sturgeon Point Road and Isle Pierre. We scouted this route for the Parks Canada Centennial Fur Brigade reenactment and managed to find sites where we could accommodate 100 campers. We had no trouble finding wilderness sites for the three tents of our scouting group. Firewood and drinking water are easily found.

Wolf tracks in the mud. Jack Wainwright photo.

- **Access:** Start at Fort St. James on Stuart Lake either at the reconstructed Fort or at Stuart River Campsite on the right after the bridge over the Stuart into Ft. St. James. Check with the Parks Canada supervisor for suggestions regarding secure parking. Take out at Miworth above Prince George at Wilkins Park; or at Fort George Park one km down the Fraser.
To get to Wilkins Park drive 16 km from the Hwy. 97 and 5th Ave. junction then up Otway road on the south side of the river to Wilkins Park. Other access points are Sturgeon Point Rd. (from Vanderhoof drive east past Chilco to the Sturgeon Point Rd.) or Isle Pierre ferry (on road maps).
- **Shuttle:** Secure parking near the take-outs may be difficult in Prince George. You may have to make arrangements with a private home owner. At Fort St. James the staff at the Fort will find some way to accommodate long-term parking. Car rentals and taxis can be had in Prince George and public telephones are in the parks. The road shuttle is 152 km from Prince George to Fort St. James on well maintained roads.
- **Maps:** You will need the National Topographic System maps 1:250,000 scale: 93-K Fort Fraser, 93-J McLeod Lake, 93-G Prince George.

The Stuart and Nechako Rivers were historically paddled by the Carrier Indians who had a village near the confluence of the two rivers and the Fur Brigades who had Forts at Fort St. James and Prince George. In 1806, Simon Fraser established Fort St. James on Stuart Lake which he had named after his second in command, John Stuart. The history of the area is well described in Parks Canada's reconstructed Fort St. James.

Most of this trip goes through an area with drier summers. July averages only 6 to 9 days with measurable precipitation. The mean summer temperature is 14 to 16° C. The waters in this general area are among the warmest in B.C.. We swam in the Nechako in July and found it quite acceptable.

Geologically, the exposed bedrocks are primarily sedimentary and date back to the carboniferous epoch which predates the age of dinosaurs. The surface features are those of a wide valley and show the contours of two ancient glacial lakes that existed after the last ice-age some 12,000 years ago. One covered Stuart Lake and much of Stuart River, the other glacial lake covered much of the Nechako River. A third glacial lake covered the Fraser and McGregor Rivers around Prince George.

The vegetation is charted as sub-boreal spruce which is characterized by slow-growth trees, primarily spruce. However, there are many sawmills in the area that survive on fir and Douglas fir. The river bottoms have many areas of primary growth forest deciduous trees that grow rapidly and eventually give way to the coniferous climax forest. Logging has opened up the region with a network of roads and some ranching is going on in cleared areas. South of Sturgeon Point on the Stuart, the wilderness suddenly opens to display the Mandalay Ranch complete wih satellite dish and logging road access to Prince George.

The first hazard is encountered upon entering the Stuart River. At low water there is only one channel around an island, stay river left; at high water avoid the grade II water in the canyon to the left of the island by going to the right of the island. We had fairly high water when we ran this in July and there were two channels to the right of the island. We hesitated long enough to almost broach on a mid-stream stump. As it was, we pivoted around it and carried on as though nothing happened, much to the chagrin of the spectators waiting for a disaster.

The next seemingly million miles of river is almost currentless. Progress is slow as on a lake. You will not cover as many miles as you might have planned. After Sturgeon Point, the river picks up speed and grade II rapids and sweepers show up on the bends. The Chinlac Rapids are encountered a couple of hours past the Mandalay Ranch. The first is a series of boulders, grade II standing waves and holes....run it on extreme river right. A km downstream the second part of the Chinlac rapids is a series of ledges creating grade II-plus Rapids....run them at extreme river right. At the higher water level we had, these were pretty well washed out.

Mosquitoes did not bother us on the river, but one night we made the mistake of sleeping in an old trappers cabin as the alternative was to clear a tent site. Our concern about mice was groundless, but the mosquitoes almost carried us away. And they were active all night. Our advice to you is to pack mosquito netting and repellent.

Just before the confluence with the Nechako, there is a bluff river right with a large cleared area on it. This was the site of the Carrier Indian village which was destroyed in 1745 by a large war party of Chilcotins. It was never rebuilt. The Nechako can be silty. Half a km below the junction river right there is a good fresh water creek. Finmore is a town about 4.5 km up the Nechako. It is possible to paddle and line up to it and take out (or put in) there.

The Nechako is grade I with some grade II on the bends and mid-stream boulders until about 4 km above Isle Pierre (km 140, 142) where there are four ledges where the best route is river right. Below Isle Pierre stay left of the island. Isle Pierre rapids are about three km below Isle Pierre. Keep left of the island. Twenty km of grade I paddling brings you to the White Mud rapids of fast water and boulders. The main rapid here has large ledges extending out from river left creating several nasty reversals. There is a downstream V near the right shore with haystacks at the bottom.

Take the first set river left and the second set river right. It appears impossible to line it and the portage along the railroad track river right looks difficult. White Mud Rapids requires good moving water skills. There is some minor faster water and boulders for the next few km and then the river is grade I to the take out.

The Stuart River flows for the most part free from human encroachments. There are no railroads, roads, powerlines or homes for most of its length. As a result, this river is much the same as it was when Simon Fraser paddled it. The Nechako has a rail line but little else. Unfortunately the Nechako has been seriously affected by the Kemano dams and its flow has been cut drastically. The latest dam may reduce it to just 10 percent of its normal volume, in effect reversing its flow to Whitesail Lake and through the Kemano generators.

SHUSWAP RIVER (Mable Lake to Mara Lake)

• **Location:** East of Enderby.
• **Difficulty:** One major portage, some grade II rapids over ledges and on bends, sweepers and snags all on the upper section of the Shuswap which can be run with empty canoes. The lower section of the Shuswap is grade I with minor obstructions. Lots of lake grade paddling is possible too. Intermediate paddlers and novices with some moving water experience can handle this trip, or avoid parts they are not comfortable with.
• **Length:** Mable Lake is 30 km long, giving over 60 km of lakeshore paddling. Shuswap River below the Chucks is 37 km to Enderby and another 32 km to Mara Lake. Mara Lake is about 15 km long, giving another 30 km of shoreline to explore. Give yourself at least two days on the river and a few more days for lake travel.
• **Hazards:** On the lakes, expect powerboat waves, cold water and winds. On the river expect ledges, sweepers, log piles and standing waves.
• **Camping:** This area is getting more populated so unorganized camping may be hard to find, however, there are some private campsites, Mable Lake Provincial Park Campsite and an unorganized site on the river at Three Valley-Mable Lake Road which will allow you to vehicle camp and do the whole trip with empty canoes by day tripping.

- **Access:** To explore Mable Lake, camp at the Provincial Park,
35 km north on a gravel road from Lumby on Hwy. 6. Put in at
Mable Lake Provincial Park boat launch on the east
side of the lake. Alternatively, camp at Three Valley-Mable
Lake Road unorganized site or Cooke Creek Campsite on the
Shuswap River then shuttle to the end of the road halfway up
Mable Lake on the west side.
To get to Cooke Creek Campsite, take Mable Lake Road
North from Hwy. 97 east from Enderby. Cooke Creek Road
is 16.4 km past the turn off to Trinity Valley and
Lumby, a total distance of about 25 km and thirty minutes
driving from Enderby. At Cooke Creek Road, just past a log
house on the right, turn right onto a rough dirt road from
Mable Lake Road North to the campsite on the river.
To run the river, put in 6 km above Cooke Creek Road
at the bottom of The Chucks rapids or 4.6 km up-river
at Three Valley-Mable Lake Road which can also be a
camping area. Take out at Enderby at a public launch site river
left one km below Hwy. 97A.
To run the lower river to Mara Lake as a day trip, put in at the
Enderby take-out and take out at the boat launch at Mara Lake
Provincial Park (no camping).
- **Maps:** National Topographic System 1:250,000 82-L Vernon.
Larger scale NTS maps are also available.

There are several places in B.C. that are easily done as day trips, from one or two campsites. This is one of them. Mable Lake offers miles of shoreline to explore, more than can be done as day trips from one location. As B.C. grows, unorganized camping becomes more difficult. Land becomes private and although the beaches are public, waterfront landowners often do not see it that way. However, private campsites seem to spring up to accommodate us as the wilderness dwindles so it is never hard to find a place to camp.

The Shuswap River's Skookumchuck rapids (The Chucks) are fearsome playwater for rafters and closed boats and are no place for open canoes. In low water open canoes can handle the rapids below them. In medium water, open canoeists must be expert moving water paddlers. Open canoes should avoid this river in high water. Late July, August and September are best for open canoeing.

The Shuswap from Enderby to Mara Lake can be run by novices with some knowledge of moving water.

This entire trip area was part of a huge sprawling glacial lake as the last ice age ended some 12,500 years ago. Mable and Mara Lakes are remnants of this glacial lake as are Shuswap and Okanagan Lakes. Winds can come up suddenly on narrow Mable Lake. Summer thunder storms developing late in the day account for much of the summer precipitation. July averages 6-9 days of measurable precipitation. The climate is cooler at Mable Lake and goes through warmer transitions towards Mara Lake.

Fishing can be good in Mable Lake. Indian pictographs can be found on Mabel Lake north of the Shuswap River outlet on the west side 400 m south of the rock point at Tsuius Narrows. Watch for poison ivy when exploring on land.

This area is one of B.C.'s finer recreation areas and as a result the paddler will be sharing the water with fishers and power boaters on the lakes and lower Shuswap River, and with rafters, tubers, closed boats and fishers on the part above Enderby.

Easy Shuswap run. Marlin Bayes photo.

THOMPSON RIVER

- **Location:** Savona to Spences Bridge.
- **Difficulty:** This trip has much minor grade II water and one grade III to IV in a canyon. Intermediate paddlers and novices with some moving water skills will enjoy the Savona to Ashcroft half. Intermediate paddlers with good river skills are usually able to handle the rapids in the Black Canyon below Ashcroft.
- **Length:** Savona to Ashcroft is 38 km and Ashcroft to Spences Bridge is 35 km for a total trip of 73 km. It is another 20 km to the Frog. Allow two days to paddle the full trip.
- **Hazards:** Watch for grade II water at gravel bars, bridges and outside bends. Below Ashcroft the Black Canyon can be grade IV. Martel Rapids may have no clear channel over the gravel bars. There are no sweepers or logjams, but in high water, whirlpools can form which can suck down a canoe, so it is prudent to avoid paddling close to strong eddy lines. Below Martel it is grade II mostly with some more difficult but runnable rapids between there and the Frog. Beyond the Frog are grade IV and V rapids which are not recommended for open canoes.
- **Camping:** This river is not usually run with loaded canoes because vehicle access is relatively easy and empty canoes are more buoyant and maneuverable. Vehicle or tent camp at Juniper Beach Provincial Campsite just west of Savona, at the Martel take-out 8 km above Spences Bridge, at Spences Bridge either river right or left or at Goldpan Provincial Park Campsite downstream of Spences Bridge.
- **Access:** Put in at the Savona Beach Park in Savona. Parking in their lot for the day is secure enough. Lunch break or take-out can be at Juniper Beach Campsite. Take-out for day one is usually at Ashcroft. The take-out there is river left at a beach above Ashcroft. If you miss it, it is possible to take out at the motel above the bridge, but that access is through private property and they discourage it. Day two put-in is at the Ashcroft beach. The next take-out is at Martel, river right 8

km above Spences Bridge or river right or left just
below the confluence with the Nicola at Spences Bridge, or
another 10 km downstream at Goldpan Campsite, or 10
more km at Nicoamen River which is just above the
Frog where the Thompson turns west sharply.

•**Shuttle:** Because this trip is best done with empty canoes and
people are vehicle camping, the shuttles are obvious and vary
according to camping location. However, this trip should never
be done without the safety margin of at least three canoes. The
vehicles doing a shuttle may have to be specially rigged to
carry extra canoes. There are no car rentals or taxi services
although a local garage could probably work out some help
with a shuttle, for a price. There are services in Spences
Bridge, Cache Creek, Savona and Ashcroft.

•**Maps:** the National Topographic System map scale 1:250,000
is 92-I Ashcroft. Larger scale maps are available from NTS.

River touring. Marlin Bayes photo.

Although there is much grade I easy moving water, there is enough grade II to call this a grade II river. The Thompson is a high volume river with frequent powerful hydraulics. Some paddlers consider it is a *pushy* river with lots of currents augmenting the main flow. Watch for rough water with standing waves on bends, where the Bonaparte River enters and under the several bridges. Choose wide channels under the bridges and stay in the middle of them to avoid the strong eddy lines they generate downstream. At low water, gravel bars will present challenges. At medium water levels, all rapids are runnable. At high water, open canoes will swamp, especially in the huge hydraulics generated in the Black Canyon. To check the water level, scout the rapids at Martel about 8 km above Spences Bridge. If there is no apparent clear channel, the river is low. If there is more than one clear channel, the river is high. Also, if the old bridge pilings at the pump station upstream are barely visible, the river will be runnable. If they are sticking well out of the water, the river is really low. Major rapids occur at the Black Canyon a few km below Ashcroft. They can only be partially scouted at the entrance to the canyon. The big standing waves are generated by boulders deep enough that they appear not to exist. Open canoes will usually swamp if they run down the middle. The challenge is to skirt them and stay upright. There are a few good gentle eddies after the canyon that let paddlers rest and regroup. Canoes must have companions to assist in rescues, should not be loaded with camping gear and should have extra flotation such as air bags. The last time I did this stretch, half of our group ended up swimming. The water temperature in summer is nice for swimming. We do not recommend running this river in flood.

The Thompson River was noted and named by Simon Fraser as he passed by on his way down the Fraser because he thought that was the river David Thompson was at the headwaters of. Thompson, however, explored the Columbia and never paddled the river that bears his name. At that time there was an Indian Village of 1200 at the confluence of the Thompson and Fraser, near where Lytton is today. Of the group of Overlanders that came down the Thompson, one perished in the rapids.

This river flows through some of the driest terrain in B.C. The plateau country high on either side of the river is covered with commercial-size timber because it gets a higher rainfall than does the valley. The Thompson Valley is a desert with sage brush, cactus and rattlesnakes. The weather is generally ideal except that winds seem to always blow up-stream on nice days. We have not often seen wildlife on this river, but we did see a badger once, and that was a first. In the spring asparagus grows wild on many islands and river banks.

Geologically, the Thompson cuts through lava flows that occurred a million years ago and built the surrounding plateau. The part we paddle down to Spences Bridge was once an arm of a glacial lake which formed when the ice age ended about 12,500 years ago. The huge deposits of gravel and sand are products of the ice age glaciers. This is not considered to be a wilderness trip as the highway is often visible. The CPR and CNR mainline tracks use the valley and other human encroachments abound. The challenges on this trip are those of paddling the river.

Touring on the Thompson. Marlin Bayes photo.

Challenging Shuttle Trips

KOOTENAY RIVER Gibraltar to Wardner
- **Location:** Southeast B.C., Canal Flats, B.C.
- **Difficulty:** This part of the river is mostly fast water with clear or easily paddled channels, with at least one rapid to grade III on the last day.
- **Length:** From the put-in at the Kootenay Bridge above Gibraltar Rock to the take-out at Wardner, the river meanders about 132 km. Allow at least three days to paddle it.
- **Hazards:** Snags, deadheads and sweepers with a few easily-run rapids and one grade III rapid where the St. Mary's River enters. Scout it and run or portage river left.
- **Camping:** Camping is unorganized. Wilderness campsites can be found . As well, roads parallel the river allowing vehicle camping and daytripping with unloaded canoes. There are B.C. Forestry public campsites in the area, but none on the river.
- **Access:** From Canal Flats, go east on Kootenay River Road, which follows the river, for about 27 km to Gibraltar Rock. Put-in. at the bridge about 5 km upstream of Gibraltar Rock. Take-out at km 27, the Hwy. bridge at Canal Flats; at km 69 Skookumchuck, Hwy 93/95 bridge; at km 89 , Wasa; at km 107, Fort Steele; or at trips end at Wardner. Take out also at informal accesses where unofficial roads meet the river. Much of the river has road access on both sides. See the BC Forestry map Invermere and Southeastern BC.
- **Shuttle:** Secure parking can be arranged at most of the take-outs, but not at Gibraltar Rock. For daytrips and vehicle camping, vehicles can be left at the take-outs for the daylight hours you will be on the river.
- **Maps:** Use the National Topographic Survey maps 1:250,000 scale 82-G Fernie and 82-J Kananaskis Lakes. Larger scale NTS maps are available and give better detail. Also get the free

BC Forest Recreation Site maps for Invermere (scale 1:250,000) and Southeastern B.C. (scale 1:300,000).

The section from the bridge above Gibraltar to Canal Flats has grade II rapids although none of them are particularly difficult. Intermediate paddlers with moving water skills will have no difficulty. Below Canal Flats it is a pleasant paddle through a rural landscape.

This is a silty river, but one of the warmest in the province. Average summer temperature for the river below Canal Flats is 15.5 to 20°C. For other general details of the area see the Columbia River (upper) on page 129.

Expert paddlers may wish to day trip the Kootenay River above the Gibraltar Rock put-in. Access the river at the bridge about 37 km farther along the road, just at the southeast corner of Kootenay National Park. The river is runnable at moderate water levels and will have grade III rapids. Allow for one long day of paddling this section. BC Forestry suggests this section has the Kootenay region's best wild river qualities and the most scenic features.

Rugged Kootenay country. Cooper Graphics photo.

LARDEAU RIVER

- **Location:** North of Kaslo, B.C. on Hwy. 31.
- **Difficulty:** This river is generally grade II with sweepers, rocks and snags. It is best done as a day trip with empty canoes.
- **Length:** From a put-in at Gerrard to the take-out at the bridge near the mouth is about 47 km, however, we have not checked this river out above the put-in where the Hwy. 37 bridge crosses the river. From there it is about 12.5 km to the take-out.
- **Hazards:** The lower part we did had logjams skirting the river, snags and rocks channeling fast water, and a decent current. The outfall from Duncan Dam can be seen from the Lardeau but appears to have no effect as a hazard on the Lardeau. There are several small streams that enter on river right that have pushed a lot of rocks into the main channel creating cross-currents and turbulence.
- **Camping:** Underbrush was thick but where vehicles access the river, camping sites could be found. This trip would lend itself to vehicle camping and daytripping the river.
- **Access:** Hwy. 31 follows the path of the river and informally accesses it frequently. The access roads are dirt, can be quite rutted and puddled. Low-clearance vehicles may have problems. Put in at any of the accesses. Take out at the bridge near the mouth east of Cooper Creek.
- **Shuttle:** There is no security for vehicles left overnight along the river, which is another good reason for day tripping. Arrangements can probably be made at Gerrard but there are no dwellings reasonably close to the take-out at the mouth.
- **Maps:** Use the National Topographic System map 1:250,000 82-K Lardeau. Also the BC Forest Service Recreation Sites map for Upper Arrow, Trout, and Duncan Lakes area will be helpful for the surrounding area, although it does not list any campsites on this river. It is free and at 1:250,000 scale. Only the NTS maps will show rapids and permanent paddling hazards. Get the largest scale NTS maps available.

This river is not well known to us, it is advisable to be prudent.

From our observations, logjams will be a hazard. From our experience, log obstructions appear and disappear following freshets. They will not appear on any map. As always, when you cannot see a clear channel ahead, land and scout it out. Sweepers can usually be avoided. Strainers, on the other hand, with the current flowing through the logs, can pin a canoe and roll it under.

An interesting phenomenon observed along Hwy. 31 on the way to the river is how the hydro poles have gone formal with neckties. Apparently the local high school graduating class started putting neckties on the poles instead of defacing the area with graffitti as some others do. Hydro appears to have gone along with the idea so now, as each succeeding class graduates, more and more poles appear to go formal.

The Squamish. Martin Kafer photo.

SPATSIZI - STIKINE RIVER (Spatsizi to Hwy 37 on the Stikine)

- **Location:** Spatsizi Plateau Wilderness Provincial Park, east of Dease Lake on Hwy. 37 (Stewart/Cassiar), north of Smithers, B.C.
- **Difficulty:** This trip is for advanced or intermediate paddlers with good moving water skills. Runnable rapids to grade II on the Spatsizi and no portages after getting on the river. Jewel Rapids on the Stikine (see p. 161) requires scouting and can be run at lower water volumes. Beggerlay Canyon 129 km below the confluence with the Spatsizi must be portaged on a one km trail, river right. Prince George paddlers have run Beggerlay at lower water.
- **Length:** The Spatsizi is 92 km from the put-in to where it meets the Stikine. The Stikine is another 152 km to the take-out at Hwy 37. The total trip is 244 km. Allow at least eight days to paddle it.
- **Hazards:** There are runnable grade II rapids on the Spatsizi. Watch for sweepers and other hazards. On the Stikine, Jewel Rapids must be scouted and Beggerlay Canyon must be portaged. The best trail is now river right as a bridge has been built over Beggerlay creek and the trail improved. Other hazards include remoteness and no services. Northern Sun Tours reports that at a little canyon about 5 kms. below Klappan, a large S-bend has large standing waves with strong eddies. Be aware.
- **Camping:** Camping is unorganized. Campsites are readily found. Campfires are permitted, but BC Parks requests that they be kept small and that cooking be done on camp stoves. All refuse must be burned and packed out of the Park. Drinking water is easily obtained. Boil or purify it chemically to guard against Giardisis (see p. 225). This area can have frost in any month.
- **Access:** This is a popular trip as you can drive to within 5 km of the put-in on an abandoned railway grade. The 5 km portage is a good trail and connects the railroad grade with the put-in on the Spatsizi at its confluence

with Didene and Kluayetz creeks. People have even
used canoe carts or wheels on it. At Tatooga Lake on Hwy.
37, turn east onto the Ealue Lake Road for 22 km,
crossing the Klappan River where it then intersects the
abandoned B.C. Rail grade. The grade skirts the south-western
Park boundary for 114 km. It is rough road but drivable
for most vehicles. This access route is subject to change and
should be checked before travelling. Tatooga Lake Resort is on
Hwy. 37 at the junction. Some arrangement must be made to
get your vehicles from the put-in to the Hwy. 37 take-out at the
bridge over the Stikine. It may be possible to arrange for a
driver from the resort to shuttle your vehicles and store them
securely while you are off paddling. The RCMP detachment at
Dease Lake should be able to advise regarding reliable storage
and shuttling.

The best shuttle would be to work a co-operative venture with
RVing friends who would drive your vehicles from the put-in
to the take-out as part of their touring this wonderland by
road. The fishing and scenery are good along the Stewart -
Cassiar Hwy. The trip to Stewart and Hyder is as scenic as
anything in the Yukon or Alaska and is a must see for anyone
touring. The best concentration of bears fishing for
salmon, available to the touring RVer, is at Fish Creek near
Hyder.

•**Maps:** BC Parks puts out a free brochure called Spatsizi
Plateau Wilderness Park with a scale of 1:280,000. It does
not show contours, but it does note rapids and trails. The
National Topographic System maps scale 1: 250,000 show
contours and important features. You will want 104-H
(Spatsizi); 94-E (Toodoggone River); 104- I (Cry Lake);
104-J (Dease Lake). See the next trip **Stikine River - Upper**
for more information about the last half of this trip.

STIKINE RIVER (Upper: Tuaton Lake to Hwy. 37)

- **Location:** Spatsizi Plateau Wilderness Provincial Park, east of Dease Lake on Hwy. 37 (Stewart/ Cassiar), north of Smithers, B.C.
- **Difficulty:** This trip is for advanced and intermediate paddlers with moving water experience. Lots of grade I and grade II fast water; sweepers, rocks and fallen trees and at least four portages, some over very poor trails.
- **Length:** 112 km from Tuaton Lake to the confluence of the Spatsizi River and another 152 km from there to the take-out at Hwy. 37 for a total of 264 km. Allow least eight days of paddling.
- **Hazards:** There are impassable rapids that are a 1.2 km portage river right at about km 20 at Fountain Rapids. At km 31 (3 km below Chapea Creek) portage river left. Seven more km of fast grade II water gets you to a pink granite canyon. Scout this carefully. It is usually runnable in medium to low water but it eats logs and canoes at high water. Twenty km below the confluence with the Spatsizi River, 2-km-long Jewel Rapids requires scouting. Canoes can usually sneak through. Portaging is possible on either side. At Beggerlay Canyon, 129 km below the Spatsizi River, portage river right one km over a bridge spanning Beggerlay Creek.
  Other hazards include remoteness and total lack of services.
- **Camping:** Camping is unorganized. Campsites are easy to find. Tuaton Lake is alpine country and fragile. B.C. Parks suggest using campstoves for all cooking and, although campfires are permitted, they ask that they be kept small. Garbage should be burned, compacted and carried out. Drinking water is readily available, but B.C. Parks recommends boiling it as a precaution against Giardisis. Travel totally self-contained as there are no services in this remote land. The frost-free days for this area are only 60, so frost may occur almost any month of the year. July averages 10-13 days of measurable precipitation.
- **Access:** Tuaton Lake is accessible only by float plane. Charter flights that will fly in you and your canoe and gear are

available from Dease Lake, Tatooga Lake, Eddontenajon Lake, Terrace, Telegraph Creek and Smithers. Take out river left just upstream of the Hwy. 37 bridge over the Stikine. There are no services here, so prior arrangements must be made for being picked up, or chance leaving a vehicle here.

•**Maps:** B.C. Parks puts out a free brochure called Spatsizi Plateau Wilderness Park with a scale of 1:280,000. It does not show contours, but it does note rapids and trails. The National Topographic System maps, scale 1:250,000, show contours and important features. You will want 104-H (Spatsizi); 94E (Toodoggone River); 104-I (Cry Lake); 104-J (Dease Lake).

The Stikine River drains the Spatsizi Plateau from its source a few km upstream from Tuaton Lake all the way to the Pacific Ocean almost 500 km away. It may be paddled in three distinct trips, each one requiring different access technicalities. The other two are in this book as the Spatsizi and the Lower Stikine.

The geology of this drainage basin is varied, but basically the exposed bedrock is volcanic or sedimentary. The Tuaton Lake is dated

Running the Stikine. Martin Kafer photo.

Jurassic which means it was created 140 to 195 million years ago. The area has undergone several periods of glaciation since then which has given the area its present features. The last iceage has left most of the land, but remnants still can be found in the present day glaciers on the Coast Mountains to the west. Just below the Grand Canyon of the Stikine, Telegraph Creek just about centers the site of a huge ancient glacial lake.

The climate in this part of B.C. is cool. The mean temperature in July is less than 14° C. The precipitation is fairly evenly distributed throughout the year. July averages 10 to 13 days with measurable precipitation but annual rainfall totals only 50 to 75 cm (20 to 30 in.) The Stikine River responds to rainfall patterns. If the area has a very wet June or July, the river will be high and all named rapids will have to be portaged. The river historically peaks at the end of June or early July. The best time to travel it is late August to early September when the river is lower. Tuaton Lake is over 1275 m (4250 ft.) above sea level which means frost or even snow at any time.

The area was protected as a Provincial Park in 1974 because it is rich in the indigenous large mammal population of North America and may even be one of the last strongholds for some species. Grizzly bear, black bear, wolverine, otters, mink, moose, caribou, sheep and goats live here. The name Spatsizi is from the Tahltan Indian language and means red goat because the mountain goats here habitually roll in red iron oxide turning their normally white coats red. Hunting is permitted in-season, which means problems with camp bears will be minimal. Even so, B.C. Parks recommends caching food at least 4 m high and 2 m from any tree. This is best done with ropes using carabiners as pulleys noted on page 83. Firearms should not be needed (see page 81) but pepper bear spray is available and legal for use on animals in B.C. It fires a stream from a spray can, but you have to be within 5.5 m. (18 ft.) of the bear to be effective. Obviously it will be a last resort.

The vegetation ranges from alpine meadows at the start through spruce forests at lower elevations. The combination of mountains, water, animals and land make this one of the most scenic places in the world.

Take plenty of film and a good camera or you'll wish you had.

A solo Prospector at dawn. Marlin Bayes photo.

Saltwater Canoe Camping Trips

Saltwater and tidewater are synonymous in B.C. No other canoeing is like it. Saltwater paddling provides all the rewards and challenges of lake and river canoeing and a whole bunch of new ones. The challenges are big league too. You will face the same conditions as commercial fishermen, powerboaters and sailboaters. And you will be in a craft that is more at the mercy of the currents and less visible than any of them. You will however always have an option the others do not have. When they have to run to safe haven, you need only land on shore, pick up your boat and walk in to shelter.

Getting lost on a river trip or a B.C. lake trip is rather hard to do. After all the river only goes one way, and lakes are surrounded by land so if you follow the shore you eventually get back to start.

Tidewater however is not the same. Currents run as fast as any river and can carry you out to sea.

A Deer Group Sea Cave. Martin Kafer photo.

Islands can all look the same and if you try to follow a shoreline, you may simply end up circumnavigating an island which brings you back to where you got lost in the first place. Sea fogs often form in the summer obscuring landmarks. Finally, canoes or any other similar low craft are virtually invisible to radar. A B.C. Ferry captain took us up to the bridge and demonstrated just how invisible we are to radar. Then when we took our halibut boat shuttle down the Queen Charlottes and watched as the one-man operator set a course by chart then left the boat on auto-pilot while he mended his nets on the stern deck, we realized that no matter how visible we were, it did not count if no one was keeping watch.

The key to safe saltwater tripping is as always, anticipating and preparing for the worst. We have previously outlined the points to consider in canoe camping in general. They all pertain to saltwater tripping plus the following new ones.

To avoid getting lost, be certain to have the navigation charts for your area and learn how to read them. These charts note landmarks and navigation aids such as lights and channel markers. Take a decent magnetic compass and a calibrated straight edge if the compass does not have one. With these, you can accurately plot your location and plan the best route to take. Knowing where you are is important. If a fog rolls in you can still plot a course and paddle on. Often a fog is there because the wind is not and so you may want to take advantage of the still seas to move on. Fogs also come and go. We have found the outer islands of the Broken Group fog-bound while those closer to the mainland were basking in sunshine.

The charts will note channels, channel markers and current speed and direction. These are particularly important for a slow moving craft

Through the sea arches. Martin Kafer photo.

such as a canoe. Knowing that you are about to cross a marked channel used by commercial boats and knowing that your survival hinges on avoiding any collision with a powered craft, means that you will be especially alert and looking far up and down the channel anticipating any powered traffic that might overtake you before you get across. And you will not dally in the channel.

Currents in channels are tricky things to anticipate. Slow currents in narrow channels will not have much effect. Slow currents in wide channels can throw a canoe way off course. If your canoe is crossing a 2 km wide channel at a cruising speed of 4 km /hr. and the current is 1 km /hr., you will be a km off where you were expecting to go. Fast currents have a much more profound effect in wide channels and in narrow channels they can have all the characteristics of a very serious river rapid.

The charts indicate current direction and speed. Do not ignore them. We did once with near disasterous results. A group of experienced paddlers camped at Porlier Pass at the north end of Galiano Island with the express purpose of analyzing whether we needed a different instructional course other than our moving water one for ocean currents. We found that we could play in the currents and read them the same way as we read river currents. We then decided to ferry across the channel to Valdes Island and play there for awhile. We ignored the fact that a strong current was moving us out to sea faster than we were crossing. No problem, we thought, we will just paddle back when we are beyond the current's effect. Wally Priedolins and I were the end canoe. Halfway across we heard a roar, glanced over our shoulders and saw a huge whirlpool opening up just off our starboard stern. You never saw two guys paddle harder in your life. We both knew our lives depended on it. That was the kind of eddy that sucks down boom logs. We knew if we capsized we would have to swim down into it in hopes of getting spit out quickly. We both knew, too, that we would probably not be able to hold our breath that long. The others heard our yell, saw what was happening, but of course were powerless to help. They watched as we pulled free, got sucked back in then finally, slowly, pulled free. Moments later a very small whirlpool opened up in front of us. We had momentum and so elected to dash through it. Small as it was, it whipped us around, but couldn't suck us down. We learned something that day and it may be significant that Wally and I collaborated on the first Saltwater paddling course for the BC Recreational Canoeing Association. Wally Priedolins is now the recognized authority for these courses and has taught and led many paddlers on saltwater trips.

Another bit of BC canoeing lore is how a choppy sea got renamed. A group that Wally was leading had been pinned down by weather. The seas were too rough to paddle safely. Wally is an early riser and knows that paddling early in the day avoids the afternoon winds. On this day, Wally, a Latvian, was first up. He walked out to the point to check the sea conditions. Then he roused all the others declaring that the channel was like a mill pond. Everyone jumped into high gear and they were off just in time to meet the wind and more choppy seas.

Poking into nooks and crannies. Martin Kafer photo.

From that day, a choppy sea is known to B.C. paddlers as a Latvian Millpond.

Currents are "sometime" things. They come and go depending on the tides. These things depend on the position of the moon, and to a lesser extent, that of the sun and so are never at the same time or strength from one day to the next. Books of tide tables and currents are published each year. Vol. 5 covers Juan de Fuca and Strait of Georgia. Vol. 6 covers the rest of the B.C. coast. On a rising tide, water flows through constricted channels into bays and inlets, creating currents that flow like rivers. Skookumchuck Rapids on Sechelt Inlet are awesome grade IV rapids in full bore, yet at slack tide a novice can paddle through them. On a falling tide, the water surges back out to sea as the currents reverse their direction of flow. The science may be exact, but the information printed, while fine for powerboaters, is not good enough for paddlers.

What happens in fact is the tables are based on selected points and the user must then estimate what time and effect will be operative where he is. Because currents can have such an effect on paddlers, small errors are magnified. We have, at times, found ourselves paddling harder and longer than we had estimated because we had not been accurate. There can be as much as two hours difference between tide and current in Johnson Straits. The problem is only serious when you cannot get back to camp because a strong current in a channel is running against you. If you are daytripping from a camp, it is often prudent to pack up the gear just in case you can't make it back. Daytripping from a set camp means plotting a course that will have the currents with you or at least not impeding you.

We almost had that problem on a Gulf Islands trip. We paddled with the current to a B.C. Parks campsite on Gabriola and set up camp. What we did not know, until evening, was a change in policy. The site was posted at the road as no camping. We had come by water. The RCMP ordered us off, but reconsidered after we pointed out that we could not paddle back until after the tide changed and by that time it would be too dark to see and paddle safely.

Tides are not the problem for paddlers that they are for powerboaters. We do not have to worry about how to get a beached craft back in the water. Nor do we have to anchor in deep water. We can pull in and land just about anywhere we choose. It is wise to check the charts for water depth and bottom. It is no fun to pull in on a high tide and find that in the morning you have a half km slog through soft oozy mud to load and launch. It is also disconcerting to find that the nice beach you landed and camped on is under water at high tide. Reading the tide tables and examining the last tide lines on the beach will help you choose dry campsites. Wally misscalculated on a northern Vancouver Island trip though. His camp was high enough according to the tide tables, but he had not counted on a wind that pushed the water higher during the night. In the morning they paddled the beaches trying to recover their gear that had floated away. Luckily they had pulled the canoe up high enough and tied it down because it was right side up and full of water in the morning. Had it not been tied, they would have lost it.

It is seldom that you will ever get flat seas on the open waters around B.C. There is always a swell of some sort. Ocean swells are not a concern far enough off shore as your canoe simply goes up and down as the swells flow under you. And the crests of these are so far apart that an 18 ft. canoe will never encounter more than one at a time. Where they become a concern is when they approach shore. As the water gets shallower, the waves shorten and crest to become breakers which can capsize a canoe. Waves then rebound off the rocks and when they arrive from different directions they can create a very localized choppy sea, even when the wind is not blowing. The lee of an island may have quiet water and give safe landing while waves break and rebound on the other three sides.

Communications are possible on saltwater trips that are not possible elsewhere. Sony's Weatherman is a receiver that is tuned to the radio band that transmits the latest weather conditions. ELT's are Emergency Location Transmitters that are used to transmit the location of downed planes, marooned sailors and ships in distress. A satellite scans the earth frequently, picks up the signal and transmits it to Search and Rescue units. A compact marine radio transceiver will allow you to talk with the Canadian Coast Guard from just about any place on the coast. This device, though, requires a licenced operator. The test is relatively easy and does not require the knowledge of morse code. For further information call Communications Canada or drop into a local radio shop.

Now, why would anyone want to face the elements by saltwater tripping? The answer is because it is unique and exciting. The excitement arises partly out of the conditions that may arise but also out of the new experiences you have. Nowhere else have we paddled through natural arches and tunnels. We have landed on beaches that seldom feel the foot of man and beachcombed for the flotsam and jetsam from other lands and ships at sea. We have paddled into caves and had startled cormorants diving from their cliffside perches into the sea around us. We have explored these caves and stumbled on Indian burial sites. One cave held 14 human skulls. We touched nothing and left subdued and reflective.

We have had whales surface nearby, watched sea lions on their rocky islands, spotted our coastal dolphins and talked back to the harbour seals. Otters and sea otters are a constant thrill. The birds that we see are specialized for that habitat and are seldom seen elsewhere. Oystercatchers, gulls, guillamots, auklets,...the list is a long one.

Fishing, crabbing and clamming can be excellent. On some trips just a few rods have provided so many fish that the others pleaded to be let off the steady fish diet. We have eaten just about everthing that moved on the beaches, and many things that did not. Even gooseneck barnacles went down well as Happy Hour hors d'oeuvres. Wally is fond of saying that the sea will provide everything you need if you will just look for it. So on a Deer Islands trip, we had deep fried fish and chips. Wally found a huge kettle and had brought a gallon of cooking oil. Rockfish were caught, filleted and battered. Ten lbs. of potatoes were distributed, peeled, and sliced into chips. An open driftwood fire got the oil to temperature and driftwood tongs got the food in and out, deep fried to perfection.

A caution is in order. We live with regulations. Before a trip, check the fishing, crabbing, and clamming regulations and get the necessary permits. Conservation officers show up in the remotest places. Also know how to recognize red tide and its effects.

Red tide is a bloom of a micro organism that colours the water rusty red. It is worse in quiet bays where it is not dispersed by wind and waves. It is ingested by filter feeders such as clams and oysters and may linger in them well after the visual effect in the water is gone. Eating bivalves or snails so contaminated can be deadly. The first effects are a tingling of the lips. A healthy person can survive a bit of red tide but not a massive dose. The rule to follow when there is no other evidence of red tide is to eat only a tiny amount and wait to see if any symptoms occur. If none occur, it is probably safe to eat more. Because red tide comes and goes, you may find areas posted as closed due to red tide (or PSP which is Paralytic Shellfish Poisoning) and then watch as the locals collect and eat them with no ill-effect. Crabs and fish are not affected by red tide.

Dogs have been known to jump out of canoes or upset them when a seal surfaced close by. For this reason paddlers should think twice about taking a dog on a saltwater trip.

Now, knowing the foregoing, there are some basic rules to follow for all saltwater trips.
1. Carry navigation charts, compass, tide and current tables and know how to use them.
2. Always check for powerboat traffic far and near before attempting to cross a major channel. Never dally. Always keep the group tightly together to minimize blocking a channel and to maximize your visibility. Never presume the powerboat is watching. Realize you are invisible on radar.
3. Paddle in the lee of islands or far enough off-shore to minimize wave action.
4. Check your campsite for both high and low tide conditions.
5. Understand and respect the power of currents, winds and waves.
6. Consider carrying an emergency electronic communications device.
7. Get all the necessary permits and regulations before you go.
8. Be wary of paddling with a dog in a canoe.

BUILD A SAUNA ON THE BEACH
1. Erect a framework of driftwood, paddles, etc, just big enough to sit in.
2. Cover and seal it with plastic sheeting or a big tarp.
3. Build a big campfire and heat bread loaf size rocks in it.
4. Use a shovel to bring the hot rocks into the sauna.
5. Sit in the sauna; splash water on the hot rocks.
6. Sweat, then dash into the cold ocean ....invigorating!
CAUTION: Some water-soaked rocks like shale may explode when heated.

Saltwater Common Trip Details

All our saltwater trips have things in common which are listed below and will not be repeated for each trip. The maps that we included are just to give you a general idea of how sheltered or open a trip is and show options for exploring that are generally too numerous to list. They should not be used for navigation.

Any hazards we list are specific to that trip and are over and above all those outlined in the last chapter.

We have noted before how far you can go in a day, but it bears repeating. A loaded canoe draws about 13 cm of water and is a displacement type hull. That means that while you can cruise through the water at an easy paddling pace, paddling at sprinting speed will exhaust you and you will not go much faster. Canoes recommended for canoe camping generally are as long as is reasonable, because the extra length will let you cruise faster. Plan on a speed of about four km per hour. If you are a mere mortal and paddling with a group, you will probably stop every 90 minutes or so.

On a river you can rest and drift and still cover the miles. Rest on the ocean and you will go wherever the wind decides to take you.

Considering that you will probably have several false stops looking for a campsite and you want to stop before dark, it is probable that you will comfortably cover only 20 km per day. We covered 15 miles or 24 km one day and because of the stops looking for campsites found it to be a long, hard grind. The return trip went faster because we knew where we were going to camp. The point is, you should not overestimate how fast or how far you will go on any given day.

None of these trips requires a shuttle. Security for vehicles may be arranged if anyone lives near the put-in, but more often there will be several vehicles left unattended in the same area. Even if yours is the only vehicle there, make sure it is out of the way of other potential users even if you have to walk some distance back to the put-in. If they decide to grade the road and you've parked on the travelled portion, you might have to bail it out of an impound lot.

Leave details of your trip with relatives so they can notify authorities if you do not return as scheduled. The starting point will be where you left your vehicle. If it is gone, they may assume you returned and moved on without notifying anyone. Leave a note in your car of your probable route and the color of your canoe. In most cases such information may be left with the RCMP too, but in our experience, that is often inconvenient and far from fool proof. The police have more to do than keep track of paddlers on vacation.

Finding drinking water can be a problem on saltwater trips. Always start with at least two full collapsable 10 l. plastic containers. When one is empty, start looking for replacement water.

First time canoe campers may have difficulty finding water, oldtimers don't. The normal instinct of looking at the map for streams does not work well on our coast. Often these larger streams drain water that has oozed out of the mass of decaying vegetation of our coastal rainforest and is stained a coffee brown colour.

The best drinking water we have found often comes from small seepages along the shore. It is generally clear and a lot more appealing to drink. Always treat it to destroy micro-organisms before using it. These seepages are usually spotted by the unusually green vegetation in the area. The flow is often too gentle to fill containers. The routine is to scoop out a reservoir and use a small cup to fill the larger container. Some of the trips do discover reliable sources of water that may have served an Indian village or an early homesteader.

Skirting the line. Marlin Bayes photo.

Saltwater Trips (No shuttle)

BROUGHTON ARCHIPELAGO (Blackfish Sound)
- **Location:** Alert Bay to Echo Bay.
- **Hazards:** Apart from the conditions always present on saltwater trips, you must be very alert to the conditions created by currents when crossing some of the channels on this trip. Cruise ships and other marine traffic use Blackfish Sound. Beaches to land on are frequent enough, but tent sites are not easy to find.
- **Length:** Alert Bay to Echo Bay, touring and exploring as we did was about 50 km one way. There are hundreds of islands and sheltered waters to paddle. We took ten days which included enforced stops due to windy weather conditions and planned layover days.
- **Camping:** Good campsites are few and far between. We needed space for five tents. Some sites found would handle one or two tents only. Firewood is plentiful, drinking water is not. Even Echo Bay water is stained brown. We found campsite #1 in the Pearse Islands on the east end of the one above the island marked elevation 245. These islands were not named on our chart which is the reason our description is so convoluted. This site was small but adequate. The Indian Reserve on island elevation 295 in the Plumper Islands could be used in an emergency, but the small boaters have been using it for bathroom stops, and not too discretely either. Across Blackfish Sound there is water and private pay camping in the bay on S. Swanson, behind Flower Island. Swanson Island is privately owned and paddlers have encountered problems with the owner and her dogs. Farewell Harbour Yacht Club is in the bay on the west side of Berry Island. They display a big sign saying "Members and Guests Only". Mound Island just north of huge Harbledown Island has a great campsite on the SE

corner which is getting over-used. About 17 km north of Mound, Insect Island has an excellent site on its south point. In Echo Bay, a local kayaker went over our charts and noted other good sites: one on Alder Island near Mound; one in the middle of the Burwell group; one at the end of Waddington Bay. As we said, campsites are few and far between. It is possible to use the campsites as base camps and tour the islands on daytrips as there are a lot of islands to explore. The Indians will now allow pay camping on Mammalilaculla.Carry lots of water.

•**Access:** Drive up Vancouver Island to Port McNeill. Take the ferry from there to Alert Bay. Arrange with a resident to leave your vehicle under their supervision. We doubled up canoes and left half our vehicles in Port McNeil at an impound lot. Notify Alert Bay RCMP of the details of your trip. Put in at the launch ramp at Alert Bay.

•**Charts:** Use the Canadian Hydrographic Service chart scale 1:75,000, PORT HARDY TO QUEEN CHARLOTTE STRAIT. See also B.C. Parks Coastal Marine Parks of B.C.

Outrunning the rain. Marlin Bayes photo.

We did it in mid August and started in wind and rain and ended in sunshine, which is about par for this area which is at the end of Queen Charlotte Strait. The average annual rainfall is less than the west coast of Vancouver Island, but is still up to 150 cm, which is 5 feet of rain. Summers are driest, but July still averages 10 to 13 days of measurable precipitation. Mean temperatures for July average 14 to 16 °C. which is the second coolest range for any part of B.C., but it is still tolerable.

The bedrock exposed on these islands is mainly granitic intrusions dated at less than 140 million years and is similar to most of the B.C. mainland coast bedrock. They were scoured of the younger rock over them by the actions of iceage glaciers which reached a depth of 1500 meters in this area. Although these low elevations were exposed over 12,000 years ago, remnants of the glaciers still exist in the mountains of the Coast Range to the east.

The area is temperate rainforest with hemlock, cedar, firs, Douglas fir and spruce predominating in coniferous forests that clothe the slopes. The area is being logged, but has never been industrialized with sawmills or pulpmills. Undergrowth is often a thick tangle of salal which makes finding campsites difficult.

Fishing has always been important here. The commercial fleet harvests mostly salmon and herring. Recreational fishers are very important to maintaining the economy in this area as can be surmised by the number of small planes frequently flying overhead to fly-in lodges. Recreational touring to see the area or view the whales by paddle power or hired powerboats is increasing.

Blackfish Sound is part of the protected inside passage route for cruise ships and freighters plying the B.C. coast, but the rest of the islands are free of such traffic and largely uninhabited. In fact, after we left Alert Bay, we did not see a home on shore until the Indian Village on Health Bay and the village at Echo Bay. The rest of the area has no permanent inhabitants.

We saw bear, deer, mink and otters on shore. We thrilled to see a pod of killer whales as we crossed Blackfish Sound and were a bit apprehensive when a 25 foot minke whale surfaced within a few meters of our canoe. Dahl porpoises were spotted, sea lions roared at night and harbor seals swam by. The fishing was good for salmon and rockfish, but we did not catch any crabs of legal size.

Mound Island and Insect Island campsites are ancient middens as evidenced by their white shell beaches. Mammalilaculla is an abandoned Indian village. Totem poles and house poles are there both standing and fallen. It is well worth visiting. The Indians have watchmen there and will allow pay camping. Take your camera. New Vancouver, south of Mammalilaculla, is another abandoned native village. It has good water. Indian Affairs bureaucrats decided that the natives would have to consolidate their villages into one at Health Bay, if they were to receive any government benefits, and so these two sites became historical monuments.

From the Insect Island campsite, we took a day trip around Baker Island, had lunch at Muffin's Cafe in Echo Bay, then fished and caught salmon on the way back along the north side of Baker. The big teepee we found on the Insect Island camp belonged to Muffin and her husband. They brought it out from Ontario, lived in it for a few years and still go back occasionally.

Whale watching in the Archipelago. Martin Kafer photo.

BROKEN ISLANDS

- **Location:** Barkley Sound, Vancouver Island.
- **Hazards:** The Broken Group of Islands is extremely sheltered paddling water, but there is about 8 km of fairly open water to paddle to get there. The Broken Group is away from commercial marine traffic channels.
- **Length:** To get to the Broken Group from the put-in at Toquart Bay is about a 10 km paddle and usually takes about two hours. A few more hours will get you to the outer islands. From one camp there you can make daytrips exploring and circumnavigating islands. From a base camp on one of the inner islands, you can make similar exploratory daytrips. A week is not long enough to see all of this area.
- **Camping:** As this is part of Pacific Rim National Park, camping is allowed in designated sites only. Park wardens patrol in inflatables and will order you off if you camp elsewhere. We have seen them order people off the beach at 5 pm when there was no where else for them to go. There is no way of knowing in advance if a designated tent site is full or not, as people can come from any direction to get there. The Parks Canada station is on Nettle Island, away from the usual canoe route. Carry water and stoves. Water may be replenished at the campsite on Willis and on Clarke. There is good water but no camping in the bay NE on Effingham. All the designated camping sites will soon have $19,000 solar powered composting outhouses.
- **Access:** Most paddlers put in at Toquart Bay, paddle between the Stopper Islands then over to Hand Island as the most sheltered way to go. To get to Toquart Bay, take Highway 4 from Port Alberni west towards Tofino. As you pass Kennedy Lake, watch for a good gravel logging road on the left about halfway down the lake with signs saying McMillan Bloedel, Kennedy Lake Division. Take that road south several km, pass Mabel Lake. As the ocean comes in to view, you will get a scenic vista of the nearest islands. Proceed to the end of the road onto an alluvial fan that has a boat launch ramp and

probably dozens of cars and campers. This is Toquart Bay. You may camp, park and launch here free. Pit toilets are provided. There are no services. The Lady Rose has a regular run from Port Alberni and Ucluelet to the abandoned Sechart Whaling Station north of Nettle Is. Some paddlers take their canoes over that way and start exploring in totally sheltered waters.

•**Charts:** Use Canadian Hydrographic Chart 3627 BARKLEY SOUND AND APPROACHES. Also get Parks Canada's map on campsite locations and their latest regulations. The B.C. Forest Service Map for Port Alberni shows the road to the put-in.

This area is temperate rainforest. The annual precipitation exceeds 250 cm (over 8 ft. of rain), however summer is the dry season with an average of only six to nine days of measurable precipitation in July. Mean daily temperature for July averages less than 16° C. Highs seldom exceed 24° C. Sea fogs and scotch mist can roll in and make everything damp and cold in summer. The undergrowth is thick with salal and evergreen huckleberry, both of which are harvested for the florist industry. The ocean stays cold and you will not find much urge to swim in it. Bioluminescence often exists so when you throw a rock in the sea when it is pitch dark, the water may emit light.

Exploring Effingham Island. Jack Wainwright photo.

The Broken Islands has history. The coast was the transportation route for early people. Anthropologists have documented progressions of people from those that carved petroglyphs whose origins are now lost, to the natives that were living and warring all up and down the coast when the first European explorers arrived. These food-rich islands must have had a long history of habitation for if you watch for stinging nettles as you paddle by these islands, you will identify the sites where they lived. Nettles like an alkaline soil and they thrive on the ancient middens of huge mounds of shells, the garbage dumps of a primative people, which now mark their ancient village sites. It is illegal to dig in a midden without the proper permits.

Check out the abandoned Indian village site at the beautiful beach on the NE side of Effingham. A walk through the area will disclose the remains of several longhouse sites. In many places, beaches were hand-cleared of rocks to make better landing sites for their canoes. Look for them. Salal Joe was the last official inhabitant of the islands. His garden was on the east side of Dodd.

The first European to visit was Captain William Barkley in 1787, a private trader on the brig Imperial Eagle. He traded with the Indians on Effingham and he and his wife named many of the places. In 1788 Captain John Meares arrived and renamed many locations.

Indian reservations were established in 1882 on Nettle (Cle-ho) and Effingham (Village Reserve). John Benson settled on Benson Island in 1893. Fruit trees and a meadow mark the site.

Six major ship wrecks have been recorded since 1870. In 1972 the 8500 ton Vanlene sank in 180 ft. of water off the east side of Austin Island with a cargo of 300 Japanese automobiles. She showed at low tide for a long time but has now slipped deeper into the water.

In 1973 the Broken Group of islands became phase two of Pacific Rim National Park.

The bedrock is mainly metamorphic schists and gneisses of undetermined age. They were exposed and sculpted by the ice age glaciers, the last of which receded over 12,000 years ago. Although these ice flows stopped at the ocean, they were still 600 m thick over these islands. The ocean continues to shape them as you will see from the many caves on the exposed shores. Follow the trail on Benson to a blowhole. Check out the tidal pools on Benson and other islands. Canoe through the natural bridge on SE Effingham.

There are no bears but look for deer and mink on the shores, otters cavorting in the bays, and sea lions on the east side of Wouwer. At low tide, search for spiney sea urchins, goose neck barnacles, myriad sea stars, whelks, limpets, sea cucumbers and more. Take a good seashore reference book and plan to paddle at low tide along the lee side of the outer islands. Beachcombing can be good and so can the fishing.

BUNSBY ISLANDS

- **Location:** West side of Vancouver Island, west of Zeballos, B.C.
- **Hazards:** In addition to the general hazards of saltwater paddling, there is 8 km of exposed coast to paddle. This is open ocean paddling and will always experience swells and difficult landings. There are other islands such as the Mission Group to explore if the swells are too much.
- **Length:** From the put-in at Fair Harbour to the first campsite on the Bunsby Islands is 50 km, excluding exploring bays and islands. It is usually paddled in three days. Allow at least a week to paddle and explore the area plus layover days if the wind comes up.
- **Camping:** Camping is unorganized. Sites are not too plentiful. Carry drinking water. Upon leaving Fair Harbour, your first night can be near Trail Creek just west of Surprise Island in Crowther Channel. Camp two can be on the mainland peninsula directly north of McLean Island. This is the start of the open water dash north to the Bunsbys. Day three campsite can be near the southeast tip of the small island as you enter the south end of Gay Channel, which is pretty much the first sheltered paddling you get to. Use that camp as a base to take day trips exploring the Bunsby Islands and nearby lands. Return using the same campsites.
- **Access:** From Zeballos drive to Fair Harbour. Arrange to leave your vehicle under supervision there and put-in there. Another access at the mouth of the Artlish River at Tahsis Inlet is a shorter drive and a bit longer paddle. To find it, use the B.C.

Forestry Recreation map: From Hwy. 19 turn on the road to Zeballos, then go right at Atluck Lake (five campsites). Follow the good logging road west to the end of Atluk Lake and then south, over a pass to the Artlish River. The road follows the river to tidewater.

•**Charts:** Use the Canadian Hydrographic Service chart for the area. Get the largest scale available. B.C. Forest maps: Port McNeil Forest District and Campbell River Forest District.

The Bunsby Islands may be more suited to closed boaters like sea kayakers, but open canoeists with spray covers do it successfully too. There are many miles of coast to explore there. Our club members have stumbled on Indian burial locations with human skulls. We caution you to not disturb any artifacts of that nature. We know of one who did pick up a skull, and the rest of his trip was steady rain. That is not a force to annoy, especially when you have a bit of open water paddling to get back! A totem pole was seen on the SE corner of Byers Cone Indian Reserve. Water was found up the creek in Battle Bay. There is a cabin and a smokehouse in the big bay on East Bunsby Island.

One of the unique animals in North America is the sea otter. They were wiped out in B.C. long ago by the fur traders' demands for their premium pelts. The last population of them was found off California but now they have been successfully reintroduced to their old range off the B.C. coast. One reason for touring the Bunsbys is to see sea otters in the wild in their natural setting for they are now naturalized there. They are also in abundance around Spring Island.

This is temperate rainforest country where the annual rainfall ranges from 250 to 350 cm. That's approximately 8 to 12 ft. of rain. The mean for July is 10 to 13 days of measurable precipitation and that is the dry season. January has more than 22 such days. The cold water of the Pacific Ocean moderates the land temperature, so this area has July temperatures of less than 14°C which is as cold as any place gets in the summer in B.C....and in January it is the warmest with mean temperatures over 5°C.

Kyuquot is a village sheltered by the Mission Group of islands with a grocery store and bed and breakfast accomodation.

DEER ISLANDS

- **Location:** Across the channel from Bamfield, Vancouver Island.
- **Hazards:** There is one fairly busy channel to cross to get from Bamfield to the Deer Group. It generally takes about 45 minutes to cross this 2 km gap. The islands and the channel often experience summer fogs and are subject to winds. This channel, Trevor Channel, is the natural route for anyone using the popular Alberni Inlet. Commercial marine traffic and powerboaters are numerous in Trevor Channel and the deeper waters around the islands. There is a lot of sheltered canoeing around these islands.
- **Length:** This chain of six main islands is only about 20 km long, but it will take at least three days to paddle around them. A week is not too long if you are exploring the small beaches and caves.
- **Camping:** Camping is unorganized. There is good camping on Diana Island near the NE corner and near the south tip. From Diana, you can explore all the southern islands on day trips. Good campsites are also found on the small islands south of Fleming Island and on the Stud Islets. Good water and a poor campsite are found in Holford Bay on Tzartus, across from the Stud Islets. There is also water in Sproat Bay on the SE edge of Tzartus Island. There are no good campsites on the east side of Tzartus. Note and avoid camping on Indian Reserve lands unless you get their permission. During the Alberni Canal salmon run in late August, the campsites are crowded with tin-boaters, fishers with small aluminum boats.
- **Access:** Drive to Bamfield on Vancouver Island. Put-in at the public boat launch ramp.They are charging a few dollars to launch at the ramp. Carry to the beach to avoid the charge. Park off the travelled part of any unposted road in Bamfield, or pay at a parking lot. During fishing season, ramp space and parking are at a premium. There may be no charges off season. Services are available in Bamfield.

•**Charts:** Get the Canadian Hydrographic Service chart: 3627,
British Columbia, BARKLEY SOUND AND APPROACHES.
This chart is scale 1:77,918 At this scale a nautical mile is 7/8
in. or 2.3 cm. Five cm is approximately 4 km on this scale. It
is actually 2.5 percent short but for day canoe trip planning, it
is adequate.

Apart from the usual exploring experiences, check out the
following. There is a sea lion rookery on Folger Island that you can
paddle into on calm days. The NW side of the Chain Group and
Fleming has numerous sea caves and tunnels. Take a flashlight.
Beware of cormorants catapulting into the sea all around you in some
of those narrow channels. Helby is mostly private property.

It was at the Stud Islets that we had our impromptu feed of fish and
chips. Fishing is not too bad, but it took two rods all day to get enough
rockfish to feed a dozen hungry paddlers. This area is world famous
for its salmon fishing.

DESOLATION SOUND

•**Location:** North of Powell River.
•**Hazards:** Malaspina entrance can be a two-knot current.
Desolation Sound can be windy with landing sites limited due
to steep terrain. Check ahead on your charts for landing
beaches in Desolation Sound and Redonda Island.
•**Length:** From a put-in at BC Parks Okeover Arm campsite and
launch ramp, it is possible to day trip the two main arms of
Malaspina Inlet. The old portage trail from Wooton Bay at the
end of Lancelot Inlet that used to let canoeists get over to
Portage Cove on Desolation Sound and make a circle trip
around Gifford Peninsula, is now privately owned and posted
no trespassing...don't plan on using it, but you can always
ask. Watch out for loose guard dogs. Most of the rest of that
peninsula is park. If the weather is not windy, paddlers can go
the 45 km up Waddington Channel and Pendrell Sound
at Redonda Island, wilderness camping on the way. It is easy to
spend a week exploring. Add more days to swim and fish.

- **Camping:** The put-in at Okeover Arm BC Parks Campsite has five vehicle campsites and four wilderness sites. Desolation Sound Marine Park is a day use area and has five tent sites. Copeland Island Marine Park west of the area has wilderness tent sites. Roscoe Bay Marine Park on Redonda Island has wilderness campsites. Carry drinking water and camp stoves.
- **Access:** The only access for canoeists is at the BC Parks Okeover Arm boat launch. To get there take Hwy. 101 north from Powell River towards Lund. Watch for signs to the Park. From Hwy. 101, it is another 5 km on paved road.
- **Charts and maps:** BC Parks map of Provincial Parks of the Lower Mainland also Coastal Marine Parks of BC. National Hydrographic Service chart 3594 Discovery Passage and Toba Inlet.

This area is very popular with powerboaters and as a result will not give you the feeling of wilderness paddling that so many other BC trips do. It is popular for good reason. It has the warmest saltwater in B.C. which means it is good swimming in summer and great spawning grounds for warm water loving oysters as can be seen from the many oyster farms there. Fishing can also be good. Malaspina Inlet and the other inlets near Okeover put-in are fairly well sheltered from wind. It is also within powerboat range from Vancouver.

Powerboaters may send you some waves in narrow channels, but the speed limit in Malaspina Inlet is limited to 4 knots to protect the oyster operations there. At Roscoe Bay on Redonda you can portage into 2.5 km Black Lake for good trout fishing. There are logging operations, both new and old which have left roads and artifacts for you to find and explore when you don't want to paddle.

AVOID DISTURBING WILDLIFE AND PLANTS

- Every year seal pups die because they often panic and drown when disturbed.
- Disturbed seabirds fly off their nests and gulls gorge on the unprotected young.
- Many plants are protected species. They may not thrive in home gardens and may also be endangered.

GULF ISLANDS

- **Location:** Off SE Vancouver Island
- **Hazards:** There are some very strong currents in the narrow passes between islands which can generate strong eddy lines and whirlpools. They can be minimized by paddling close to shore and by going well out to sea when crossing them. Do not try to cross at the narrowest points. Check your tide charts and current tables on day trips to make sure you will get back to camp on favourable currents. B.C. Ferries routes must be avoided. Many powerboaters use the area.
- **Length:** The Gulf Islands stretch in a band along SE Vancouver Island for 100 km. You can spend a day or a month paddling and exploring.
- **Camping:** The islands are to a large extent privately owned, but forestry companies own large tracts and people often wilderness-camp on them. B.C. Parks has established a large number of parks thoughout the Gulf Islands. Some are day-use only, some are vehicle accessible and allow camping, some are accessible only by water and many of those permit tenting. Carry stoves and drinking water. Check current regulations regarding campfires. Camping is permitted at the following Marine Parks: #75 D'Arcy Is., #275 Sidney Spit, #132 Isle-De-Lis, #239 Princess Margaret Is., #20 Beaumont, #42 Cabbage Is., #260 Ruckle, #189 Montague Harbour, #330 Wallace Island, #80 Dionisio Point, #338 Whaleboat Is., #233 Pirates Cove, #209 Newcastle Is. The numbers are those given by B.C. Parks and are used to locate them on any B.C. Roads and Parks map.
- **Access:** Access points for canoe campers are found all over the Gulf Islands and on Vancouver Island. There are public accesses to the beaches wherever the terrain allows, and in Canada no one can own property below the high tide mark. The high water boundary is usually defined as where live, woody vegetation persists naturally. You may have problems leaving your vehicle unsupervised overnight in high population areas. It would be wise to arrange with a resident to pay park on

private property even if you have a bit of a walk back to your put-in. Check in with the local RCMP regarding leaving a vehicle unattended as they will run a licence check and perhaps tow a vehicle that appears abandoned.

•**Charts and maps:** National Hydrographic Service Chart 1:40,000 #3310 small craft charts of Gulf Islands. B.C. Roads and Parks Map.

The Gulf Islands lie in the protection of Vancouver Island and as a result has a remarkably mild climate which some cartographers have called "Mediterranean". Although the islands get up to a meter of rain annually, the summers are the driest in B.C. with only 3 to 5 days of measurable precipitation in July. The mean temperatures for July are a comfortable 16 to 18°C. Even January is mild, with mean temperatures up to 5 degrees and 14 to 17 days with measurable precipitation.

The predominant forest tree is Douglas fir but many others thrive too, especially the arbutus which is our only evergreen broadleafed tree. It has the unusual habit of shedding its bark rather than its leaves. The flora of the Gulf Islands is unique.

The exposed bedrock is primarily sedimentary rock laid down 25 to 140 million years ago during the Cretaceous Period. Some volcanic rock and coal deposits of the same age are also evident. The southern two thirds of Saltspring Island has exposed sedimentary rock that has been dated much older at 230 to 570 million years. The area was submerged below sea level with the weight of the ice age glaciers and is still rising slowly, resulting in the many cliffs seen along the shores.

The ice reached depths of up 1500 m here. Flying over the Gulf Islands, one is impressed with the long parallel grooves left by the moving glaciers in the bedrock, especially visible at low tide.

The softer sandstones have often been further eroded by wave action as the cliffs grew resulting in shallow caves and hollows, carved pedestals and aesthetically pleasing rounded sculptures now all high enough above tide to be free of marine growths. The climate and sandstones also limit the growth of trees in some areas resulting in park-like moss, grass and flower-covered slopes that just beg to be lazed upon.

The farther north one goes, away from the influence of the cold water coming in from the Straits of Juan De Fuca, the warmer the water is. Protected bays can offer swimming in the summer, but it may be cool. They all have intertidal marine life quite different from that found on the west coast of Vancouver Island. Beachcomb to find and identify the wide variety of life there, but leave it in place. If you turn over rocks, turn them back because not to do so smothers the life that was on top and destroys the shelter of those below. It is especially important to practice good conservation in these high-use areas if the indigenous life is to remain. Through ignorance, we have wiped out areas once rich in intertidal life around Vancouver and as far as Point Roberts. The Gulf Islands are under increasing people pressure and as a result, their rich marine life is also endangered. Regulations are in effect for the harvesting of edible species such as oysters and clams but there is far more there for the naturalist in us to get excited about. Fishing can be excellent for salmon, rockfish, and dogfish. Children will particularly enjoy fishing for shiner perch around any wharf. Use a small hook on a short hand line with a piece of mussel as bait and watch the action.

The campsites are mostly marine parks accessible by water only and there is no reservation system or guarantee that you will get a tent site. It may be more comforting to arrive early, get a site and then explore that area and surrounding islands on day trips. We have done just that. The danger is that you will head out through a channel with the help of a current and then find it against you when you try to return. The currents such as those reaching 8 knots in Gabriola Passage are strong enough to even give small powerboaters the same problem.

The thought of lining or portaging the canoe back does not take in to account the incredibly slippery algae covered rocks at lower tides, or the often impassible bluffs at higher tides. It was in Porlier pass between Galiano and Valdes that Wally Priedolins and I almost met a watery grave in a whirlpool. There is no question that the casual paddler will have problems. You must have and use the charts and tide and current tables for your paddling area if you are to have a safe enjoyable camping trip. Also read pages 189 to 198 for more understanding of the overall problems facing saltwater trippers.

ROBSON BIGHT

- **Location:** South of Port McNeil on Vancouver Island.
- **Hazards:** This trip follows the fairly exposed coast of Vancouver Island, south along Johnstone Straits which is a major commercial route for freighters. Shores are steep and landing sites can be some distance apart. Wind can be a problem.
- **Length:** From a put-in at Telegraph Cove east to Robson Bight is about 16 km which is a day's paddle. Allow at least two paddling days.
- **Camping:** Camping is unorganized. Try the creek south of Blinkhorn Peninsula. There is space along the way and at Robson Bight, but regulations now bar camping at Robson Bight in an effort to minimize disturbing the whales. Carry drinking water. Firewood is plentiful.
- **Access:** Drive south of Port McNeil to Telegraph Cove. Park and put in there. The Forestry map will help with other roads and campsites.
- **Charts:** Use the same one as for Blackfish Sound. Canadian Hydrographic Service chart PORT HARDY TO QUEEN CHARLOTTE STRAIT. B.C. Forest Recreation map Port McNeil Forest District.

This three day trip can be done as an extra trip following the Blackfish Sound excursion. The reason for going, of course, is to see killer whales in their natural environment. Since this area was identified as an important socializing place for killer whales, more and more people have gone there to see them, resulting in regulations and rules to keep the whales from harrassment.

Robson Bight is called the rubbing rocks because the whales seem to enjoy rubbing on them, and while they are not always present, they are seen there more consistently than elsewhere.

All the other data pertaining to Blackfish Sound also pertains here. However, because this area is not as sheltered, wind can be an important hazard factor.

MORESBY ISLAND

- **Location:** Moresby is the big island making up the south half of the Queen Charlotte Islands.
- **Hazards:** There is one headland to paddle past otherwise this trip is in fairly sheltered waters. Should a southeast wind come up, Juan Perez Sound can be quite rough. The area is remote with no permanent inhabitants.
- **Length:** The trip from Moresby Camp to Burnaby Island was about 100 km and it took our Halibut boat the better part of one day. The canoe trip back covered 135 km which we spread over 7 paddling days. Plan on having a few layover days to explore and fish....or to sit out stormy weather. Take another few days to tour Graham Island.
- **Camping:** Camping is unorganized. Beaches and campsites are not too hard to find although we did spend one night at the end of a logging road which was not too aesthetically pleasing. Burnaby Island has good campsites on the NE corner at Section Cove; on the west side above Dolomite Narrows and on the south shore. We found other sites at the point just before entering the south side of Hutton Inlet; in the Bischof Islands; near Lyell point on Lyell Island; near Magee Point on Talunkwan Island's south shore; and at the logging road at Trotter Bay. Weather did not allow us to get to Hotsprings Island, which is posted No Camping. Nearby islands have campsites. There is a B.C. Forestry campsite at Moresby Camp, the starting point. Carry water.
- **Access:** Take the ferry from Prince Rupert to Skidegate Landing near Queen Charlotte City, then the free ferry across to Moresby. Drive past Sandspit and follow signs another 40 km or so of gravel road to Moresby Camp at the head of Cumshewa Inlet. This is the usual starting point for paddlers as it cuts out a full day of paddling Moresby's exposed east shore. There is no security for vehicles left as no one lives there. However, it is a well-used site with a gravel launching ramp and wharf. Security does not seem to be a problem as there are always vehicles left unattended there. If you wish to charter a

boat as we did, there are several to choose from as tourism is an important source of income for the islands. Try Kallahin Expeditions 559-4746 or yellow page listings for the area will put you on to an outfitter who can help.

•**Charts:** Use Canadian Hydrographic Chart #3853 for the best scale. NTS map 1:250,000 103B,C Moresby Island gives elevations and details for hiking but it stops just short of the last few km into Moresby Camp. The B.C. Forestry Map is scaled 1:500,000, but it is helpful in that it shows logging roads. The B.C. Road map at a scale of 1:2,500,000 just shows main roads.

Upon leaving Prince Rupert, the majestic snow-capped Coastal Mountains fade and sink on the horizon before the green hills and cloud cover of the Misty Isles ever begin to show. The Queen Charlotte Islands are made up of two main islands, Graham in the north and Moresby in the south and myriad smaller ones. The main spines of the islands are the Queen Charlotte Ranges, but they rarely top 1500 ft. with The Twins at 1838 ft. on Burnaby Island being the highest on the trip. The tree line ends at about 1500 ft. so members of our group that took a side trip to climb Yatza Mt. were rewarded with a view of the Pacific coast side of Moresby Island and were into alpine flora.

Moresby Island morning. Marlin Bayes photo.

One look at the rounded hills tells you that they did not escape the glacial scouring of the ice age glaciers. Scientists tell us that here the ice reached heights of about 900 m so even the highest mountains were covered. The glaciers that covered B.C. extended over the Charlottes and ended abruptly at the Pacific Ocean where it now laps on the western shore of Moresby Island. The scouring exposed the bedrocks we now see. South Moresby is older volcanic and sedimentary rock dated at 195 to 230 million years ago which is a time dinosaurs roamed, while the more northern part of Moresby has younger sedimentary and volcanic rocks dated at 25 to 140 million years old, which spans the time that the dinosaurs died out and mammals appeared in greater numbers. Maybe Eohippus the Dawn Horse of North America roamed here. Certainly the

Quiet Queen Charlotte fauna. Marlin Bayes photo.

climate was different, for Graham Island has small deposits of coal which formed in the steamy swamps of a sub-tropical environment. Tasu on Moresby's west coast has copper and iron deposits.

The Misty Isles comes by its nickname honestly. If it is not raining, it is probably going to, or the Scotch Mist will enshroud and soak everything. Clear days are rare we were told, so we were fortunate to have mostly sunshine and only a little rain on our trip there. Locals told us that a good day was when the clouds obscuring the hills stayed up there. We were told that we could expect to encounter all weather from mist to sun to squalls...and we did, sometimes all on one day. The drier summer months of July and August are the best time to go.

The Pacific ocean moderates the temperatures to the extent that January has a mean of +5°C. while July has less than 14 degrees. The average annual rainfall is up to 250 cm (over 8 ft.) and July, the dry season, gets 10 to 13 days of measurable precipitation. This is probably the only place in the world that a tree without chlorophyll could survive to maturity which is just what the Golden Spruce on Graham Island has done.

The soils are infertile podzolics that have been leached of nutrients by the heavy rainfall. However, the land is clothed in forests of hemlock, cedar and spruce, so in this respect the area is similar to the tropical rainforests. The trees as we saw them near tidewater were a decent size and we thought they were old growth forests until we discovered the remains of hand logging operations. Huge stumps had springboard cuts, yet the surrounding forest had recovered and healed wonderfully. On our trip down we had passed Lyell Island that had been pretty much scalped by recent clear-cutting and which became the pivotal point to preserve much of Moresby Island as a National Park Reserve in 1988. A walk on the islands on Moresby's east flank is through deep mosses, not the salal and salmonberry you expect and get elsewhere on the west coast. The area is often called the Galapagos of the north. It does appear to be different. In the early years, logging could only take the best, most accessible timber and the forest could recover, and has done so to the extent that they could selectively harvest it again. The clearcutting methods of today have stripped the

Low tide in the Queen Charlottes. Marlin Bayes photo.

hillsides, exposing the mossy undergrowth to unaccustomed elements which kills it and accelerates leaching and erosion in this land of heavy rainfall.

These islands have a place in history only because the earliest explorers came by sea and the land claims of three countries overlapped here. The Russians were working their way down the coast, claiming territory for the Czar. The Spaniards had crossed Mexico and had travelled up the coast. The British had come overland with trading companies establishing posts and claiming land for England along the way. In 1774 the Spaniards sent Perez to investigate rumors of Russian traders. He sailed as far as the Queen Charlottes but bad weather turned him back. Had he gone a bit further he might have found the Russians at the mouth of the Stikine River. In 1776 England sent Cook on his search for the Northwest Passage. In 1778 he saw and passed the Queen Charlottes and turned back at the Bering Sea. Private traders such as Meares arrived in the 1780's and had a lucrative trade going with the Indians for Sea Otter pelts. In 1789 the Spaniards sent Martinez north to deal with the interlopers. He seized a fort and ships at Nootka Sound. When the British found out, they sent Capt. Vancouver to establish their claim, almost declared war on Spain and through diplomatic channels, recovered the seized lands. They got compensation and an agreement that limited the Spanish northern claims. Meanwhile, Alexander Mackenzie reached the Pacific overland in 1793 on the mainland across from the Charlottes. The Russians established themselves on the coast and when the Czar sold Alaska to the Americans, this area went with it as the Alaska Panhandle. The Queen Charlottes were named in 1785 by a fur trader, Capt. Dixon, after his Queen and his ship of the same name.

Even though there was that flurry of historical interest, the islands have not become heavily populated. The records do not even show any commercial sawmills. The timber is cut and the logs are shipped elsewhere. The fishing banks around the islands, especially the sound between them and the mainland are arguably the best on the Canadian West coast after Barkley Sound. Large catches of herring, halibut, salmon and other ground fish are made, but surprisingly are not processed there. In the days of small canneries there were some on

Moresby but they are abandoned ruins now. There is one ruin at Lockeport and another at Pacifico Bay. We saw signs of industry and attempts at homesteading but all were abandoned and we saw no permanent residents on Moresby south of Louise Island.

The Haida Indians traded furs with the European traders and got metal and other trade goods. They also caught foreign diseases which decimated their numbers. As a result they abandoned villages and still do not inhabit them except to staff them with watchmen who conduct tourists through the ancient ruins in the summer. Visitors must have permits to visit. Ours were purchased at the Haida Band office in Skidegate. The village at Tanu has house posts, mortuary poles and deep pits where the storage basements of the dug-out homes were. The Village of Ninstints on Anthony Island is a UNESCO World Heritage site as it contains the best record of standing totem poles in the world. Ninstints is off the southwest tip of

Moresby Island totems. Heinz Prosch photo.

Moresby and is out of reach of canoes as there is too much risky open water paddling to get there. Skedans is on the east side of Louise Island and is reachable by canoe in good weather.

You must have reservations on the ferry from Prince Rupert. We shared the considerable expense by doubling up and taking only half the vehicles across. We had also made arrangements to have a boat take us from Moresby camp to Burnaby Island from where we explored for a few days and then spent a week paddling back to the vehicles left at Moresby Camp.

There are no grizzly bears but the black bears grow large. We only saw one and he did not bother our camp, even though there were bear tracks all around the campsite. The deer, on the other hand, are dwarfed blacktails about the size of a German Shepherd. They eat what they can get. There are open sites where the small hemlocks have been browsed to the point where they look like topiary shrubs. We even saw them browsing on seaweed. Racoons and otters are also there, but it is the sealife that really fascinates.

There were twelve of us in our canoeing group, but only four fishing rods. The fishing was so good that the others pleaded to be let off the steady salmon diet, and then off the rockfish diet. At low tide at Dolomite Narrows the sealife with leather stars, moon snails and other intertidal life was fascinating. There we caught more legal-sized rock crabs than the group could eat. Good thing we never caught one of those 100 lb. halibut.

Getting drinking water was not a problem for us as we each arrived with two full containers and then filled up at an abandoned homestead on south Burnaby Island where the water flowed clear and cold from a plastic pipe. We also got some from the Indians at Tanu. Finding campsites for our large group was not an impossible task either.

Weather was our main concern. It can blow up suddenly and you do not want to be caught out in it wallowing along with loaded canoes. We did elect to cross Juan Perez Sound when it was choppy with whitecaps. We all had fast canoes and when we put our backs to it, we made the crossing in what has to be a record 21 minutes (yeah, somebody timed it!). That crossing measures 5 km on the map...maybe his watch stopped. In any event we all had waves breaking over our spray covers and rain pelting down blinding us ...or was that sweat? We stopped in the Bischof Islands, found tent sites, built a fire and after the rain ended, dried out. We had already decided not to risk paddling the much farther distance to Hotsprings Island in those conditions, and so we missed it.

We went on to visit Tanu and then tackled the open water around Tangil Peninsula, which is unavoidable if you want to get back to Moresby Camp. When we did it, it was dead calm and because it was we ended up ahead of schedule and could have had time to visit the hotsprings we had passed up. So, we camped early and went fishing and exploring as the rest of the trip was all sheltered water and in all likelihood weather could not delay us.

On our return up Cumshewa Inlet we had a brisk tail wind so we lashed canoes together, hoisted a tarp and sailed back to the launching ramp.

There is no point in arriving on the Queen Charlottes and not exploring Graham Island. Not to be missed are: the Golden Spruce, St. Mary's Spring, Agate Beach, Balance Rock, Tow Hill, Naikoon Provincial Park, Old Masset, Haida Museum and artisans.

You can also take a side trip to Rennell Sound on the west side of Graham Island. The road is gravel and quite steep as it gets down to tidewater. There are forestry campsites and it is quite easy to launch your canoe over the beaches and spend some time exploring the sheltered east end. Access it through MacMillan Bloedel's camp at the end of the paved road west of Queen Charlotte City.

Moresby Island paddling. Marlin Bayes photo.

International River Classification

GRADE I	Small and regular waves; passages clear; occasional obstructions like sandbars and bridge pilings. Suitable for novices in open Canadian canoes and kayaks.
GRADE II	Rapids of medium difficulty; passages clear and wide with occasional boulders in stream. Suitable for intermediate paddlers in open Canadian canoes and kayaks.
GRADE III	Waves numerous, high, irregular with rocks and narrow passages. Advance scouting usually required. Canoes will ship water unless equipped with spray covers and will require frequent bailing. Suitable for advanced paddlers in open Canadians and kayaks.
GRADE IV	NOT suitable for open canoes. Long difficult rapids; powerful, irregular waves; large boulders. Advance scouting is mandatory. Suitable for expert paddlers in closed canoes and kayaks.
GRADE V	NOT suitable for open canoes. Very difficult, long and violent rapids; large drops; steep gradient. Advance scouting required but difficult to do so because of the terrain. Suitable for expert paddlers in closed canoes and kayaks with professional leadership.
GRADE VI	NOT suitable for open canoes. Difficulties of grade V carried to extremes. Nearly impossible. Very dangerous. Suitable only for expert paddlers in closed boats at favorable water levels and after careful study, with fully-trained and experienced rescue teams in position.

NOTE: Rapids may not extend all across a river. If there are grade IV rapids in the middle but there is room to bypass them, they will be downgraded to the kind of water you have to paddle through. If you do not have the skills to move your canoe into the quieter water then you might find yourself swimming in a grade II rapid.

Rapids are also downgraded a bit if there is sufficient slow water below them to allow a rescue. Conversely, very cold water, remoteness from services or insufficient slow water for rescues will cause a grade II rapid to be upgraded to grade III.

Grading rivers is a very imprecise art. Grades of rapids change at different water levels. Generally, it is unwise to attempt any B.C. river in flood due to the speed of the river, the lack of beach to pull out on and the unforgiving cold water . Freshets may bring trees and logs that are not on any map.

Running the Blackwater River. J.Voss photo.

Purifying Drinking Water

To make any water source as safe as municipally treated water, treat it following these guidelines produced by the U.S. Department of Health, Education and Welfare.

Use liquid chlorine laundry bleach. Read the label to determine the percentage of chlorine available.

Available chlorine:	Number of drops to be added	
	to clear water:	to cloudy water:
1%	10 drops/quart	20 drops/quart
4-6%	2 drops/quart	4 drops/quart
7-10%	1 drop/quart	2 drops/quart
unknown %	10 drops/quart	20 drops/quart

Mix thoroughly then let stand for 30 minutes with maximum ventilation. If you cannot detect a slight chlorine odor after 30 minutes, repeat the process, let stand for 15 minutes and the water will be safe to drink.

Use tincture of Iodine as an alternative to chlorine.
2% available Iodine: add 5 drops per quart to clear water or 10 drops per quart to cloudy water. Let stand for 30 minutes, after which the water will be safe to drink.

SWEETENING THE FRESHWATER CONTAINER

To clean up a container that is tainting the water, kill anything in it with a maximum dose of chlorine then dump it out. Now dissolve a heaping tablespoon of baking soda per 5 gallons of fresh water in the container. Mix it by shaking vigourously. Let it stand a few hours, then flush it and refill with untainted water.

B.C. Paddling Clubs

Canoe Clubs

Beaver Canoe Club	Burnaby	Diane Abrey	275-2704
Caribou Chilcotin	Williams Lake	E. Carnes	392-6344
Chase Secondary	Chase	Al McLean	679-3218
Columbia Canoe Club	Nelson	Eric White	825-4352
Dene Voyageur Society	Quesnel	D. McCulloch	747-2470
Dogwood Canoe Club	Vancouver	Bob Watt	988-4277
Island Paddlers	Ganges	W. Priedolins	537-4631
Kamloops Canoe Club	Kamloops	Alan McKnight	374-6870
Kelowna Canoe Club	Kelowna	Terry Miles	764-7137
Komoux Valley Paddle Clb	Comox	A. Gear	339-0292
Nanaimo Paddlers	Nanaimo	Lynne Reeve	390-4471
New Caledonia	Vanderhoof	G. LaBrash	567-4653
N.W.Brigade	Prince George	R. Brine	964-7400
Valley Paddlers	Abbotsford	L. Bell	853-5528
Victoria Canoe Club	Victoria	S. Constable	382-6581
WW Paddlers Network	Vancouver	L. Merchant	731-4767

Whitewater Kayak

Bulkley Valley Kayak	Smithers	T. Goodacre	847-4904
Bubbliscious Boaters	Elkford	B. Whitney	423-6494
Campbell River WW	Campbell River	Box 2160 V9W 5C9	
Capilano WW	Vancouver	P. Coles	985-0318
Ft. St. John Paddlers	Ft. St. John	R. Potter	785-7855
Kamloops Kayak Club	Kamloops	A. Stradeski	374-7018
Malaspina Kayak	Nanaimo	D. Cohen	758-7460
N.W. Brigade	Prince George	R. Tysen	562-1975
Vancouver Kayak Club	Vancouver	R. Sheppard	879-8028
U. Vic Kayak Club	Victoria	P. Kirschmann	592-0009
Vernon WW Club	Vernon	T. Bowen	542-7062

Sea Kayak

Sea Kayak Association of B.C.		M. Sixta	597-1122

Flatwater Canoeing Association

Kamloops	Kamloops	D. Forsythe	573-3832
Fort Langley	Fort Langley	C. Chappel	888-4396
Burnaby Canoe/Kayak	Burnaby	W. Edwards	290-9885
Chase Kayak Club	Chase	B. Smith	679-3791
False Creek Club	Vancouver	A. Lee	685-9866
Ridge Canoe/Kayak	Maple Ridge	A. McLean	463-8889
Nanaimo Racing Club	Nanaimo	B. Croft	390-2165
Duncan Canoe Club	Duncan	L. Mandziuk	748-4938
Whistler Canoe Club	Whistler	J. Callahan	932-5101
Chilliwack	Chilliwack	P. Gagnon	793-9030

Recreational Canoeing Association of B.C.
Executive List

President
Carey Robson
4782 Fernglen Drive,
Burnaby, B.C. V5G 3V7   437-1140

Vice President
Wally Priedolins
140 Mt. Baker Crscent,
RR2, C-41 Ganges, B.C. V0S 1E0 537-4631

Secretary
Tynke Braaksma
957 Hendecourt Rd.,
N. Vancouver, B.C. V7K 2X5   987-3879

Treasurer
John McBride
3629 Doncaster Drive,
Victoria, B.C. V8P 3W7   477-9435

Instr. Coordinator
John Hatchard
957 Hendecourt Rd.,
N. Vancouver, B.C. V7K 2X5   987-3879

Memb. at Large
Nola Johnston
7887 Cambie St.,
Vancouver, B.C. V6P 3J1   h. 327-3622 w.684-5747

Environmental
Juerg Boschung
4377 Southwood St.,
Burnaby, B.C. V5J 2G3   433-9314

NOTES

NOTES

NOTES

NOTES

NOTES